Google Cloud Digital Leader Certification Guide

A comprehensive study guide to Google Cloud concepts and technologies

Bruno Beraldo Rodrigues

Google Cloud Digital Leader Certification Guide

Group Product Manager: Preet Ahuja

Publishing Product Manager: Suwarna Rajput

Senior Editor: Runcil Rebello

Technical Editor: Rajat Sharma

Copy Editor: Safis Editing

Book Project Manager: Uma Devi

Proofreader: Safis Editing

Indexer: Manju Arasan

Production Designer: Prashant Ghare

Senior DevRel Marketing Executive: Linda Pearlson

DevRel Marketing Coordinator: Rohan Dobhal

First published: March 2024

Production reference: 2080324

Published by Packt Publishing Ltd.

Grosvenor House

11 St Paul's Square

Birmingham

B3 1RB

ISBN 978-1-80512-961-5

www.packtpub.com

This book is an ode to Sinhá Moreira, my great aunt, whose vision and generosity should be an inspiration to us all. She helped establish a technical school in her hometown of Santa Rita do Sapucaí in the state of Minas Gerais in Brazil. Her impact, helping people transform their lives through education and technical skills, was deeply motivating when considering this project, and I hope she would be proud of this effort as an extension of her work. I would also like to thank my parents, without whom none of this would be possible. Their appetite for risk, in pushing us to move from Brazil to Canada and eventually the US, was foundational in helping me develop into the person I am today. Lastly, and definitely not least, I'd like to thank my daughter, Lily. You are the light of my life, and every smile helps me push a little harder.

– Bruno Beraldo Rodrigues

Contributors

About the author

Bruno Beraldo Rodrigues is a technology aficionado focused on helping business and technical leaders adopt Google Cloud. He's certified as a Google Cloud Digital Leader and currently works as a cloud field sales representative, managing relationships with customers and prospects for Google Cloud. He has experience working with clients across North America, ranging from early-stage start-ups to large, traditional organizations. This work has exposed him to several industries such as healthcare, e-commerce, agriculture, security, and logistics. He's also passionate about entrepreneurship, having volunteered as a mentor with Google for Startups Accelerator programs for several years across GTM strategies and cloud architecture.

Bruno is based in Austin, Texas, and graduated from Texas A&M University. He's a proud Aggie who holds two bachelor of arts degrees, international studies and French. Bruno would also like to thank Bard, Google's generative AI chatbot, for helping him think through the content and format of the different chapters.

About the reviewer

Austin Ciamaricone spearheads the Strategic Startup team at Google Cloud for the central US, dedicated to aiding emerging leaders in scaling and disrupting their markets. He led the National Customer Success team for top customers on Oracle Cloud before joining Google in 2018 as a customer engineer, supporting key digital native clients nationwide. His unwavering objective is to enable and propel innovative technology, empowering companies through state-of-the-art cloud and machine learning solutions.

Table of Contents

3

Understanding the Different Cloud Computing Models   29

Part 2: Innovating with Data and Google Cloud

4

The Role of Data in Digital Transformation   47

5

Google Cloud Solutions for Data Management   57

Part 3: Infrastructure and Platform Modernization

11

IT Operations in the Cloud   135

12

Resource Monitoring and Application Performance Management on Google Cloud   141

Part 5: Practice Exam Questions

13

Sample Questions: Exam Preparation   151

Preface

The **Google Cloud Digital Leader certification** is a great entry point into the Google Cloud ecosystem for both business and technical folks. This book is designed to be a certification guide, walking you through the core topics covered in the Digital Leader exam while also highlighting Google's portfolio as it relates to the latest advancements in their Cloud business and services.

The book is organized into five sections:

- *Introduction to Digital Transformation with Google Cloud*
- *Innovating with Data and Google Cloud*
- *Infrastructure and Platform Modernization*
- *Understanding Google Cloud Security and Operations*
- *Practice Exam Questions*

You may find material covering these different topic areas but this book strives to include both the latest updates to the Digital Leader certification content and an overview of Google Cloud's AI offerings – a topic that is becoming increasingly more relevant for both business and technology folks.

My experience working at Google Cloud for the past 5+ years has provided me with a deep understanding of cloud migrations, the challenges customers face, the debates they have with their teams, and ultimately why they make the decisions they do.

By reading this book, you'll benefit from my unique perspective as it relates to the following:

- Understanding the *why* behind cloud migrations, particularly Google Cloud
- What factors and circumstances impact decision-making when building cloud systems
- Examples and scenarios that highlight the critical thinking and knowledge required to pass the exam

Google Cloud has been recognized as a Leader by Gartner in their Magic Quadrant for Cloud Infrastructure and Platform Services in 2022 and has a fast-growing, multi-billion dollar business. Most recently, Google Cloud was recognized by Gartner as the most innovative of the Leaders in their 2023 Cloud Database Management Systems Magic Quadrant.

This highlights both Google's commitment to its Cloud division and its ability to drive enterprise-grade innovations to market. Throughout 2023, as executives and boards feel more pressure to adopt modern technologies and compete with modern companies, their business and technology teams are also being pressured to collaborate and innovate more while also taking into account security and compliance requirements.

There is a lot of demand in the market for folks with Google Cloud skills, both at the individual contributor and leadership levels. As their customer base grows, so does the demand for the product, engineering, business, partnership, and marketing knowledge related to getting the most out of the latest technologies. This book can be the first meaningful step towards formalizing your GCP skills by helping you attain the Google Cloud Digital Leader certification.

Who this book is for

This book is written to be relevant to almost anyone who would like to take their first professional step into the Google Cloud ecosystem, whether your background is in business or engineering or you are a recent college graduate:

- **Anyone who wants to certify as a Google Cloud Digital Leader**: You will find that the content follows the certification guide, making it a great resource for GCP knowledge and preparation for taking the exam.

- **Business leaders**: For founders, CEOs, VPs, and managers striving to become more technically fluent or whose company is adopting Google Cloud, this book will prepare you with an understanding of the business impact of technical decisions and what considerations should be taken into account when designing systems that will be monetized.

- **Technology leaders**: For technical founders, CTOs, VPs, and managers whose team is adopting or exploring the adoption of Google Cloud, this book will give you the foundation you need to comprehend Google's approach to the cloud, some of the platform's nuances, and its benefits. You will gain a better understanding of what factors to take into account when making technical decisions, particularly if you want to build for both security and scale.

- **Young or new professionals**: Folks who are new to the workforce or are new to the cloud industry will find this guide to be tremendously helpful in establishing a strong foundation for both cloud industry knowledge and Google's positioning in the market. You will also be exposed to critical cloud concepts such as cloud-native, the shared responsibility model, and more.

What this book covers

Chapter 1, Cloud Computing Fundamentals – An Introduction to Digital Transformation, introduces you to basic cloud concepts and terminology. It focuses on establishing a foundation of knowledge upon which the rest of the content will be built.

Chapter 2, The Shift to Public Cloud, covers the traditional approach to building infrastructure and its benefits and challenges. It also highlights the reasons behind the shift to the public cloud with a focus on the technical and business value.

Chapter 3, Understanding the Different Cloud Computing Models, compares and contrasts the different cloud computing models. This includes the traditional SaaS, PaaS, and IaaS models while also highlighting their impact on digital transformation and the shared responsibility model.

Chapter 4, The Role of Data in Digital Transformation, provides you with an introduction to data's role in digital transformation. It discusses how the cloud enables the derivation of value from data and its impact on how technology teams build data architecture.

Chapter 5, Google Cloud Solutions for Data Management, covers the Google Cloud solutions used for data management and smart analytics. You will learn the benefits and tradeoffs of the different services with the goal of being able to identify the best solution given a set of circumstances.

Chapter 6, Machine Learning and Artificial Intelligence on Google Cloud, focuses on educating you on the challenges and best practices when working with ML and AI solutions. It highlights the services available on Google Cloud while also helping you understand how they can be applied to generate value for an organization.

Chapter 7, Modernizing IT Infrastructure with Google Cloud, goes deeper on comparing and contrasting the different approaches to building infrastructure. We'll discuss legacy infrastructure, its struggles, the benefits of modernization, and different approaches including hybrid and cloud-native infrastructure.

Chapter 8, Modernizing Applications with Google Cloud, focuses on the reasons why organizations modernize and build cloud-native applications. We'll cover the different application hosting services on Google Cloud and when it makes sense to use one over the other.

Chapter 9, The Value of APIs, highlights the role of APIs in particular when building infrastructure and applications in cloud environments. We'll cover the value that APIs provide to businesses and the benefits of Apigee, an enterprise-grade solution for full API life cycle management.

Chapter 10, Google Cloud's Approach to Security, establishes a strong foundation for understanding cybersecurity. It covers key concepts, the benefits of Google Cloud, and the solutions available to help customers harden their environments.

Chapter 11, IT Operations in the Cloud, focuses on helping you understand why and how cloud operations differ from on-premises operations. We'll discuss DevOps, SRE, and the challenges they were designed to overcome.

Chapter 12, Resource Monitoring and Application Performance Management on Google Cloud, provides you a deeper understanding of the importance of uptime for cloud customers. It touches on core concepts such as monitoring, logging, and the relevant tools in Google Cloud.

Chapter 13, Sample Questions: Exam Preparation, is composed of 100 test questions to help you prepare to take the Google Cloud Digital Leader exam. The questions are broken down into three sections: basic terminology, Google Cloud services, and situational questions.

To get the most out of this book

You will need to approach the topic with an open mind, understanding that Google approaches cloud computing from a different perspective than other providers. Although it is not specifically required, you will be able to navigate the content more easily if you have a basic understanding of the following concepts:

- Traditional computing and the parts of a computer

- Operating systems

- Applications

- Traditional hosting models

Ultimately, the book is designed to help you certify as a Google Cloud Digital Leader and strives to provide the knowledge required to pass the exam.

Review the official Google Cloud documentation. Google Cloud has built a great documentation portal. You will find the following links helpful when deep-diving into specific topic areas:

Description	Link
Google Cloud's Official Site	`cloud.google.com`
Google Cloud Customer Case Studies	`https://cloud.google.com/customers`
Google Cloud Architecture Center	`https://cloud.google.com/architecture`
Google Cloud Digital Leader Overview	`https://cloud.google.com/learn/certification/cloud-digital-leader`
Google Cloud Digital Leader Exam Guide	`https://cloud.google.com/learn/certification/guides/cloud-digital-leader`

Conventions used

There are a number of text conventions used throughout this book.

Bold: Indicates a new term, an important word, or words that you see onscreen. For instance, words in menus or dialog boxes appear in **bold**.

> **Tips or important notes**
> Appear like this.

Get in touch

Feedback from our readers is always welcome.

General feedback: If you have questions about any aspect of this book, email us at customercare@packtpub.com and mention the book title in the subject of your message.

Errata: Although we have taken every care to ensure the accuracy of our content, mistakes do happen. If you have found a mistake in this book, we would be grateful if you would report this to us. Please visit www.packtpub.com/support/errata and fill in the form.

Piracy: If you come across any illegal copies of our works in any form on the internet, we would be grateful if you would provide us with the location address or website name. Please contact us at copyright@packt.com with a link to the material.

If you are interested in becoming an author: If there is a topic that you have expertise in and you are interested in either writing or contributing to a book, please visit authors.packtpub.com.

Share Your Thoughts

Once you've read *Google Cloud Digital Leader Certification Guide*, we'd love to hear your thoughts! Scan the QR code below to go straight to the Amazon review page for this book and share your feedback.

https://packt.link/r/1805129619

Your review is important to us and the tech community and will help us make sure we're delivering excellent quality content.

Download a free PDF copy of this book

Thanks for purchasing this book!

Do you like to read on the go but are unable to carry your print books everywhere?

Is your eBook purchase not compatible with the device of your choice?

Don't worry, now with every Packt book you get a DRM-free PDF version of that book at no cost.

Read anywhere, any place, on any device. Search, copy, and paste code from your favorite technical books directly into your application.

The perks don't stop there, you can get exclusive access to discounts, newsletters, and great free content in your inbox daily

Follow these simple steps to get the benefits:

1. Scan the QR code or visit the link below

https://packt.link/free-ebook/978-1-80512-961-5

2. Submit your proof of purchase
3. That's it! We'll send your free PDF and other benefits to your email directly

Part 1:
Introduction to
Digital Transformation
with Google Cloud

In the first part of the book, you will get an overview of the cloud technology industry and Google's approach. We will cover the different types of cloud solutions and their benefits and challenges. This will include understanding concepts such as SaaS, PaaS, and IaaS, their differences, and why organizations choose to move to the cloud from on-premises environments. We'll also cover what Google thinks about its global cloud network, the shared responsibility model, and the value of digital transformation with Google Cloud.

This part has the following chapters:

- *Chapter 1, Cloud Computing Fundamentals - An Introduction to Digital Transformation*
- *Chapter 2, The Shift to Public Cloud*
- *Chapter 3, Understanding the Different Cloud Computing Models*

Cloud Computing Fundamentals – An Introduction to Digital Transformation

The cloud computing revolution is impacting organizations of all sizes, across industries, and all over the globe. Fundamentally, new ways of building systems, architecting infrastructure, and managing data have created a perfect storm for the cloud, with the total market value expected to hit $1 trillion by 2032 (according to Global Market Insights at `https://www.gminsights.com/industry-analysis/public-cloud-market`). As this massive growth market continues to expand, the need for talent that is familiar with the latest technologies and innovations also grows. The need for Google Cloud talent is particularly acute, with Google being the fastest-growing hyperscale cloud provider as of Q1 2023 with a growth rate of 28% YoY and an annual run rate of nearly $30 billion (as per `https://abc.xyz/investor/static/pdf/2023Q1_alphabet_earnings_release.pdf`). This book is designed to provide a baseline understanding of Google's approach to the cloud for both business and technology professionals and prepare you to certify as a **Google Cloud Digital Leader**.

In this first chapter, we will introduce foundational concepts for cloud computing and explore Google's view of it by highlighting how Google defines **digital transformation**, along with both the business and technical forces driving businesses to adopt cloud solutions.

Here is a summary of what will be covered:

- How and why the cloud is transforming businesses
- The benefits of the cloud for digital transformation

- Elaborating on digital transformation with Google Cloud
- Describing how a transformation cloud accelerates innovation

We will cover these learnings via the following topics:

- An introduction to data centers
- The why behind digital transformation
- The benefits of digital transformation
- Hypothetical case study – Acme Inc.

An introduction to data centers

To understand where the hyperscale cloud industry is today and where it's headed, it's helpful to dig into how the industry came about. The term **cloud** refers to a system or application that is being used for a business purpose where the infrastructure for that system is centralized, typically in a location referred to as a **data center**. Data centers are warehouses specifically built for housing advanced computing hardware, networking equipment, data, and applications.

Data centers are composed of racks and racks of servers, a business term to refer to a computer, along with networking equipment, storage arrays, and cooling and power equipment, among other components. Servers themselves are typically composed of a **core processing unit** (**CPU**), **random access memory** (**RAM**), and disk, which is typically either a hard drive or flash drive to store data. The CPU is typically used for computational tasks such as solving a math problem while RAM is used to store data temporarily, typically because data is being used by an application and being transformed in some way. Disk and flash drives are used to store data for a longer period, with disk drives being a cheaper, mechanical storage device and flash drives being more expensive given that data is stored in a semiconductor chip. Servers are used to host applications that are typically either internally facing, helping employees more efficiently and effectively do their job, or externally facing, providing services to customers and partners.

When discussing data centers, it's helpful to define the different types. We'll start by understanding the traditional approach: on-premises infrastructure. On-premises is a term that's used to refer to an organization that hosts its technology infrastructure onsite at offices or other business facilities. For example, if you are a legal firm, your systems would be on-premises if they were hosted at the same location as your office. There would be a server room or several rooms at the facility where all of the systems and data are hosted for the employees to complete their work. This location would host the systems that support worker productivity and internal workflows, while also facilitating business operations.

This approach had benefits such as making it relatively easy to secure systems and applications. If all of the systems and data are hosted within your organization's physical locations, and they are not accessible from the internet, you can establish a strong security posture through physical controls such as allowing only employees to access your facilities and not allowing them to take their workstations home with them. At a small scale, this is also a very manageable approach to infrastructure given that you could operate it with a small team and troubleshoot issues by reaching out to your local IT administrators.

However, as organizations and systems began to become more complex, scale globally, and support new patterns of work, new approaches began to surface. If the legal firm, for example, were to grow to 10 offices around the globe, it would be very difficult to continue to work via distributed, on-premises systems. Each office would need its own technology, infrastructure, and IT personnel and there would need to be a way for workers across offices to work together. They would need to share data, even if it were sensitive; if perhaps the New York and London offices were working together on a case for a multinational company operating in both the US and the UK. These pressures led to the centralization of infrastructure, which is where the term *cloud* comes from.

Let's explore the two core variations of cloud hosting: **private cloud** and **public cloud**. An organization leverages the **private cloud** when a company is running environments where there is only one tenant – themselves. This may mean that it owns and operates all of the data center infrastructure itself. The company buys or leases land, manages the building, procures the servers, installs the operating systems, and manages the applications and data while also being responsible for both the physical and virtual security of the private cloud. In some circumstances, they may procure the space from a third-party vendor but they are ultimately responsible for the hardware, software, and networking infrastructure, with the space within the facility dedicated exclusively to them. Some drawbacks of the private cloud are the requirements for large capital expenditure on real estate, equipment, and operating costs, as well as the deep complexity that comes along with having to design, build, maintain, secure, and scale their infrastructure.

In contrast, when an organization leverages the **public cloud**, it offloads much of the physical responsibility of operating a data center to a third party. **Google Cloud** is a public cloud platform where developers and engineers can access infrastructure built on top of Google's data centers and networks. This enables businesses to offload responsibilities such as building and managing the physical components of the data center to specialize in what will provide value to their customers. Customers of public cloud providers benefit by abstracting away much of the complexity of managing technology infrastructure by focusing on the virtualization layer and above. This means being responsible for the virtual machines, operating systems, applications, and data to operate their businesses.

A company that operates **hybrid cloud** environments blends both public and private cloud environments. They may have their own data centers hosting internal or sensitive applications while leveraging the public cloud for externally facing applications. This pattern is common in organizations that built up their own data centers and are building new applications in the cloud or are migrating systems to optimize for the most efficient hosting strategy. In some cases, they may build a data warehouse in the cloud to consolidate and organize data from disparate on-premises systems such as sales, marketing, logistics, and fulfillment data.

Multi-cloud is a cloud computing strategy where companies use multiple public cloud providers to host their applications. This allows them to run their workloads optimally across multiple environments and vendors, reducing the risk that arises related to vendor lock-in, where organizations become restricted in their ability to innovate and negotiate cost when they consolidate their infrastructure under a single vendor. Managing environments across multiple cloud providers can be complex given the variations between the platforms and the potential required integrations. Multi-cloud is becoming more common as engineers build skills across multiple providers and vendors begin to differentiate themselves through unique capabilities, partnerships, or contracting vehicles.

With the advent of cloud computing, we've also seen the rise of a new breed of technology company: **cloud-native**. Google Cloud states the following (`https://cloud.google.com/learn/what-is-cloud-native`):

> *"Cloud native means adapting to the many new possibilities – but a very different set of architectural constraints – offered by the cloud compared to traditional on-premises infrastructure. Unlike monolithic applications, which must be built, tested, and deployed as a single unit, cloud-native architectures decompose components into loosely coupled services to help manage complexity and improve the speed, agility, and scale of software delivery."*

Another concept that goes hand in hand with cloud-native is **open source**, as it relates to how software is developed and the accompanying standards with this shift. Historically, software has been *closed source*, meaning that the code base was owned and only viewable by the manufacturer. This led to a rise in enterprise software licensing where things such as **vendor lock-in** come into play, where you are at the mercy of the manufacturer from both a cost and capability perspective, locked into multi-year contracts, and unable to implement nor change the code base based on your needs.

In contrast, open source within the realm of software takes the opposite approach. Code bases are public, and anyone from around the world can view and contribute to the code base to ensure it meets their needs. Given this novel, distributed approach to software development, there were also requirements around policies that govern what would qualify as an open source project.

Some of the key principles to open source software development are as follows:

- Transparency, allowing public access to review and deploy the code
- Open, community-centric, and collaborative development
- Meritocratic approach to contribution, driven by experts
- Freely available without licensing or cost restrictions

Organizations that adopt the open source approach to software development can accelerate the pace of innovation for their teams given that they are not at the mercy of one company to improve the code base. Employees from the organization can make feature requests, contribute to the code base, and ensure that the code improves over time.

A great example of a successful open source project is **Kubernetes**. Kubernetes is an open source software project launched by Google as a way to help drive awareness of container-based deployment methods and architecture.

Containers were a new way of thinking about how to run applications as they relate to the underlying hardware and software. In the world of virtual machines, the application, operating system, and hardware are fundamentally coupled. This means that if the hardware fails, the application also fails. Containers allowed developers to scale applications more gracefully and build more fault tolerance into their architecture and systems. It also happened to be a more cost-effective way of hosting applications given that resources could be shared across several systems to ensure maximum utilization while minimizing cost.

This shift in designing and architecting systems translated very well to cloud-native organizations, given their flexibility and ability to rapidly innovate. More traditional organizations began to adopt similar practices as they began to comprehend the value that these approaches can deliver to their business, with start-ups rising quickly and disrupting industry after industry.

The shift from private to public cloud, by offloading the responsibilities of building and managing data centers, has enabled businesses to focus on driving change that has a meaningful impact on the bottom line. Engineers who had historically been tasked with monitoring onsite infrastructure or managing databases can be repurposed to increase developer productivity, improve the security posture, or engage in R&D projects.

As we explore the forces behind why businesses have been shifting to public cloud adoption, it's helpful to start by defining digital transformation, including its importance and benefits.

The why behind digital transformation

Over the last few decades, we've seen a steady shift of businesses and systems from analog to digital. With this shift came a significant change in how companies build teams, design go-to-market strategies, and generate revenue. This shift was fundamentally a shift from paper-based processes to computing-based processes, where files and data went from being stored in filing cabinets to databases and filestores.

Imagine that you had to run a sales report to understand how much a department had done in sales over the last 10 years, growth rate year over year, and project out 5 additional years of sales. If the documents you required were on paper and scattered across three different sites, it may take weeks to collect them, analyze them, and provide the desired report. If, however, all of the data had been digitized and made available through an application, you would be able to run a report within seconds. Moving from weeks to seconds is a massive productivity boost and would enable business leaders to make faster, more accurate decisions. This is an example of the value digital transformation can provide.

According to the Google Cloud documentation (`https://cloud.google.com/learn/what-is-digital-transformation`), the official definition is as follows:

> *"It uses modern digital technologies – including all types of public, private, and hybrid cloud platforms – to create or modify business processes, culture, and customer experiences to meet changing business and market dynamics."*

The push to digitally transform is felt across organizations, as highlighted by the official definition, as it impacts not only the tools the technology team uses but also the organizational culture and the ability to deliver modern customer experiences. Engineers often have to learn new skills or completely new technologies, adapting how they've worked to address the needs of today.

There are many reasons why companies choose to go through this transformation:

- Infrastructure flexibility
- Ease of R&D
- Quantifiable innovation
- Global collaboration
- Customer value
- Agility

Let's explore these in detail.

Infrastructure flexibility

In the world of physical data centers, capacity planning and availability can be a big blocker. Having a server procured, shipped, configured, and pushed online can take days, weeks, or even months, depending on the circumstances. One of the big advantages of working with a cloud provider is that machines of all shapes and sizes are available through the click of a button. Spinning up a server, whether it's in the US, Europe, or Asia, is a trivial workflow that makes it very easy to spin up servers virtually, deploy them, and manage them. It's all done through a secure internet connection and if you decide that you no longer need something, you can spin it down to effectively stop paying for it.

Ease of R&D

By leveraging a cloud provider such as Google, organizations can quickly and easily access, test and validate new technologies as they are developed and launched. They can spin up development projects within a secure environment, ensuring that corporate or customer data won't be accidentally leaked and that they have access to the latest technology being launched by cloud providers and their **independent software vendor (ISV)** partners.

Measurable innovation

When experimenting with different services, tools, and technologies, it can often be challenging to define success criteria and costs and make the right decisions. By leveraging a data-centric approach to testing and validation, businesses can quickly iterate on their developments and make smart decisions based on the results.

Global collaboration

Working with cross-functional teams that are distributed across the globe can be an issue whenever you don't have the right tools, systems, and processes in place to facilitate the collaboration without the appropriate security and compliance controls. Through digital transformation, you can make data more accessible to people who need it, when they need it, while still ensuring compliance with existing requirements.

Customer value

The demands that come from customers are ever-evolving concerning developments in the market and associated technologies. By analyzing how customers prefer to engage, how they grow through their life cycle, and what needs arise throughout that journey, businesses can provide tailored experiences that meet and exceed customer expectations. They can find patterns and reasons why people leave the platform for example, identify the root cause(s), and implement a way to overcome those challenges proactively, thereby increasing retention and reducing churn.

Agility

Organizations are having to compete on a global scale with companies large and small to win new customers and retain existing ones. Through digital transformation, development teams are enabled to accelerate the pace at which they innovate while also being able to significantly increase the scale of their launches. Rather than having to launch a service in a specific region or city due to process or technology constraints, businesses can now build once and launch anywhere through innovations such as global cloud providers and **Infrastructure as Code** (**IaC**).

There are many reasons for a business to transform from analog, paper-based processes to digital processes. Not only will employees be more productive, but they'll be more innovative and make better decisions. Workflows that might've taken days, weeks, or months can be compressed into days, hours, or even seconds. A common anecdote for demonstrating the impact of failing to digitize is the story of Blockbuster. Blockbuster was a brick-and-mortar store where you would go to rent or buy movies and TV shows. The walls and floors were lined with shelves covered in empty VHS and DVD boxes highlighting which titles were available. Many customers had come to cherish the experience of walking through those aisles, exploring interesting titles and genres until they finally found the one – and hoped it was in stock! Blockbuster, by 2004, had 9,000 stores globally (as per `https://www.businessinsider.com/blockbuster-is-closing-forever-2013-11`) and earned $5.9 billion in revenue (as per `https://www.sec.gov/Archives/edgar/data/1085734/000119312507239499/dex991.htm`).

Fast forward to 2023 and you won't find a Blockbuster anywhere as they were digitally disrupted by Netflix. They started by competing with Blockbuster through a video-mailing service, eliminating the need to go to a physical location and be at the mercy of what was in stock, but eventually moved onto cloud-based video streaming. Online video streaming created a new way to browse and consume content, where a customer had a massive library of titles at their fingertips. Customers began to expect to be able to watch the latest release from the comfort of their homes without having to worry about whether or not Blockbuster had that video in stock. Today, Netflix continues to be a successful company, having reached $8.1 billion in quarterly revenue for Q1 of 2023 (as per `https://www.statista.com/statistics/273883/netflixs-quarterly-revenue/#:~:text=In%20the%20first%20quarter%20of,the%20corresponding%20quarter%20of%202022`). They are now facing an innovation dilemma as they face intense competition from new services such as Disney+, Paramount+, and Max.

Now that we understand why organizations are transforming digitally, let's explore the benefits of going through that transition.

Benefits of digital transformation

There are many benefits to transforming a business so that it can leverage the latest advances in computing, software, and data technologies. Whether it's launching new products or building new capabilities into an existing business, the technology space is ever evolving and the pace of innovation seems to be increasing. Companies that have implemented or were born digital as cloud-native companies have a significant advantage over those that haven't.

Whether it's going from a monolithic application architecture that struggles to serve global clients to containers, Kubernetes, and global service orchestration, or the adoption of a data warehouse to empower analytics use cases, organizations that embrace a new way of doing things can make the most of new technologies as they quickly learn, test, validate and adopt them.

According to the Google Cloud documentation, here are the main benefits of going through digital transformation:

- Modernize infrastructure
- Manage data
- Gain insight
- Break down team silos
- Solve business problems
- Realize cost savings

Let's look at them in detail.

Modernize infrastructure

Companies that transform digitally and adopt cloud-native ways of architecting systems can meaningfully optimize their hardware and software usage. By migrating away from building and managing infrastructure themselves, they can quickly and easily build systems that have evolved from the traditional, server-based architecture to more modern, service-based architecture or even serverless systems. These systems allow their engineers to automate much of the day-to-day tasks of operating and managing infrastructure through features such as auto-scaling, which dynamically scales the infrastructure up and down based on load. They also allow for global traffic routing, ensuring that customers have the best experience based on their geography and minimizing the time and effort required to build systems that scale globally.

Manage data

Data is exploding and as companies try to gain more insight into the health of their go-to-market approach and how their customers think about them, being able to capture, organize, and integrate these datasets can be challenging. Digital transformation empowers you to go from paper processes to digital processes where new tools and capabilities can be applied to store, transform, analyze, and monetize data. Organizations can ingest vast amounts of data, going from terabyte to petabyte to hexabyte scale from a myriad of different systems, regardless of whether they're internal or external.

Gain insight

Digital systems not only allow you to more easily and efficiently manage data but also facilitate the act of deriving value from the data. Companies can adopt new approaches to sharpen the focus of their business on their core value, applying things such as machine learning to provide more value to their customers and generate new revenue streams. Business leaders can also be empowered to make better decisions through higher fidelity real-time data, which gives them a better understanding of the current state of the business and what challenges it faces.

Break down team silos

The transition from paper to digital also facilitates productivity and collaboration for teams across geographies. Employees can easily find, access, share, and collaborate on files and projects at the speed of light rather than being at the mercy of paper-based processes. Customers also benefit from this as the teams that they work with can deliver more value faster relative to competitors who don't adopt modern practices. A marketing team in India, for example, might need to update a campaign for the local market. With a digital cloud-based system, a team in the US can quickly and easily upload all of the raw marketing files to a shared drive where the India team can access it to make the appropriate updates, all with the click of a button.

Solve business problems

The adoption of technology also helps organizations approach their processes and applications with a new lens. Digital systems help business leaders quickly pinpoint challenges within the organization and its engagement with customers. By equipping them with the information they need to improve how they work and engage with customers, the business can dynamically solve problems as they arise and can continuously refine its approach.

Realize cost savings

The result of implementing digital systems and modern ways of doing business across people, processes, and technology also results in cost savings. Paper-based processes are often cumbersome and expensive, requiring significant human work and can be very slow. These challenges can be overcome by implementing technology to automate away process complexity and cost. For example, through paper processes, it may take weeks to generate, validate, issue, and execute a contract. You have to engage multiple teams to put the paperwork together, validate that what is generated will pass integrity checks, and have the appropriate provisions. From there, you may have to mail or fax a contract to someone and hope that someone is on the other end to pick it up and put it through the appropriate process. Through a digital system, however, you can automate the specific contractual requirements to have them generated with the click of a button and issued for signature – within hours rather than weeks.

There are many benefits to transforming digitally, ranging from realizing cost savings, solving business problems, and breaking down silos to more technical reasons such as modernizing infrastructure, managing data, and gaining insight from that data.

Hypothetical case study – Acme Inc.

Behind many of the major technological revolutions of the past couple of decades, there were often developments in key variables making them possible; computing, networking, and data. Whether we are discussing personal computers, smartphones, or cloud computing, they were all enabled thanks to advances in the density and scale of computing resources, the availability and quality of networking, and the accessibility of data.

Before we dive into the intricacies of Google Cloud, its services, and the impact it is having on businesses, it is important to establish foundational knowledge to ensure we start on the same page. Let's frame the technological revolution by following along with a hypothetical company, Acme Inc.

Acme Inc. – its evolution from the 1980s to the 2020s

In the early days of Acme Inc., when it was first founded in the 1980s, they were selling desktop software for personal computers. They had three offices, each with their own server closet, where any required systems were installed and hosted. Most of their corporate processes were based on paper, with the vast majority of the work not being digital. Security was relatively easy to set up and manage; only the two IT folks on the team had access to the server rooms and all employees left their corporate computers at the office – they were locked down to their desks. In this world, the perimeter was well defined; everyone had to go to the office to access corporate systems and through physical security, you could generally ensure the infrastructure was secure. No one could take their computers home and IT must be onsite to troubleshoot but overall, it seemed to be working and life went on.

As time passed, Acme Inc. continued to grow and by the 1990s, they had 10 offices around the US. The IT team realized that they wouldn't be able to physically manage and troubleshoot distributed systems across 10 offices and they needed to pivot their model. They had started digitizing their processes given the needs of the business and clients. Meanwhile, finance was starting to complain about the many hardware and software purchases required to maintain the technology ecosystem. Between all of the server and license requests, they decided to implement centralized infrastructure, empowering them to purchase equipment in bulk and making life easier for the IT team by consolidating all of the infrastructure that they needed to manage in one location.

Acme Inc. implemented a data center strategy and by the 2000s, they were running a couple of private cloud locations. They adopt **VMware** and virtualization to make the most of their hardware, allowing them to maximize hardware utilization by sharing the compute resources from their servers across multiple applications. They set up a backup and disaster recovery strategy by running a **hot-cold setup** where their backup data center would help them recover from any issues with the primary location. Managing all of the corporate infrastructure, however, started to become a burden given the heavy weight and cost of running a data center. Between keeping up with all of the security vulnerabilities, ensuring hardware procurement would support future capacity needs, and also managing finance's complaints about large capital expenditures, the IT team became overwhelmed.

Thankfully, the advent of **Software-as-a-Service** (SaaS) solutions came onto the scene as organizations were looking to offload the responsibility of managing and securing infrastructure. IT can procure technology solutions that are hosted for them, empowering them to focus exclusively on permissions and data for the application while not having to worry about all of the additional layers of infrastructure that need to be addressed when you host things yourself.

Going into the 2010s, Acme Inc. adopted several SaaS solutions for their infrastructure, ranging from productivity tools such as email, HR, and finance systems. The core of what they offered, however, was still self-hosted as their desktop application was now being modernized to be offered as a service. This ensured that you would be able to generate predictable, recurring revenue (keeping finance happy) and help address the needs of your clients. Unfortunately, because their data center was still self-hosted, Acme Inc. discovered that a nation-state attacker was able to access a database that one of their admins forgot to patch. This caused much pain for IT and sales as Acme Inc. now had to navigate challenging conversations about how they manage infrastructure and had a hard time earning the trust of their customers. Fortunately for Acme Inc., there was a new computing revolution just on the horizon.

By 2020, Acme Inc. decided to migrate its infrastructure from on-premises to an **Infrastructure-as-a-Service (IaaS)** provider. This enabled the Acme Inc. team to focus less on managing and securing the lower layers of infrastructure while empowering them to focus on projects that would move the needle for their organization. Rather than managing a database, their data engineer started building out a **data lake**. They moved all of their servers from their on-premises data centers to the cloud, which enabled them to spin down those assets and sell them off.

With this capital burden being lifted, the Acme Inc. team invested in improving developer productivity and adopted a few new approaches to building code and managing teams: DevOps and microservices-based architecture. By adopting more modern approaches to launching applications, Acme Inc.'s application is now more scalable and easily improvable than ever before. They push code to production weekly and can compete with even the hottest, most well-funded start-ups.

Summary

In our case study about Acme Inc., we touched on many of the key elements driving the change we are seeing in technology from a data center perspective. The variables that are constantly in tension with building and managing technology infrastructure fundamentally are cost versus performance and distributed versus centralized. Many of the changes that Acme Inc. implemented, whether it was going from closet server rooms to mainframes to virtualization to containers, were meant to overcome challenges around finance and customer experiences. When designing cloud systems, we are constantly trading off how we can deliver an excellent experience while trying to minimize cost. We'll see this as a common theme as we explore different use cases and prepare for the exam questions; often, you'll have to think through what would be the *best* system for the job given specific technical, business, and financial restraints.

Now that we have a general sense of why organizations around the world and across industries are transforming themselves, it's time to cover foundational cloud concepts. The focus for *Chapter 2* will be on understanding why and how the cloud is adopted across different scenarios and business cases. We'll explore the benefits of cloud infrastructure, along with how networking is the foundation upon which the cloud is built.

2
The Shift to Public Cloud

There are many approaches to building infrastructure and designing systems. There is no silver bullet for how things should be architected. Depending on the use case, how the data can be accessed, and the technical requirements, it may make more sense to build a stateless application on serverless systems or to run a database on bare metal. As we work through understanding and contrasting the differences in these architectures, it's important to also provide examples of when certain approaches make more sense. Companies have been transitioning from on-premises, private cloud infrastructure to cloud-native, public cloud infrastructure, but this doesn't mean that everything should be stateless and serverless. Depending on the architecture of current systems, what performance thresholds are required relative to cost constraints, and other factors, ultimately, customers will make the decision based on individual workload needs and the business value they need to derive from those workloads.

In *Chapter 1*, we covered foundational concepts for understanding how data centers are classified, the technologies and concepts driving cloud computing adoption, and digital transformation. In this chapter, we'll explore the drivers behind public cloud adoption. We'll also dig into how Google Cloud stands out relative to other clouds, in particular as it relates to the global Google networking infrastructure.

Here is a summary of the topics that will be covered:

- The value of adopting public cloud
- The impact of cloud adoption on finance teams
- Private, public, or hybrid?
- An introduction to networks
- Public cloud with Google Cloud

The value of adopting public cloud

At first glance, running a private cloud on-premises is a great way to build technology infrastructure. The company would have ownership and control over the land, capacity, and power requirements to ensure that they can plan for and meet the needs of their future customers. You can forecast future capacity requirements, work with vendors to develop a procurement plan, and work with customers to commit to using the future capacity.

One of the common themes that comes up with customers who have taken this approach is the idea of control. They can control where infrastructure is deployed, what application is running on that infrastructure, who can access the data center, and what hardware is used to deploy that infrastructure. However, with control and choice comes complexity and cost. Although they can choose routers, switches, and servers, does that nuance truly matter to the business? At the end of the day, the business just needs the application to load and process data quickly, and many organizations found themselves having to manage a behemoth of a problem as they scaled. Between data regionalization requirements, global collaboration, and competition from start-ups, this approach was tough to scale as quickly and cost-effectively as the business was demanding.

As technology leaders began to value developer productivity more and more, the traditional physical infrastructure procurement model began to break down. All of a sudden, developers needed servers all over the world, with unique architecture requirements at the click of a button. They didn't have time for the IT team to take 4 to 8 weeks to source the servers, have them mounted on racks, and make them available to them.

IT departments felt like they were caught between a rock and a hard place; they had to deliver capacity faster than ever before in increasingly complex environments while also being told to mature their security practice and minimize risk.

The concept of a hyperscale, public cloud provider must have seemed too good to be true and it's taken a while for legal teams to understand the implications and value of these kinds of environments. We'll dive deeper into the different approaches to cloud computing and the **shared responsibility model** in the next chapter, but businesses can derive a lot of value from public cloud. Let's explore some overarching themes.

Flexibility

When building your infrastructure and managing your data center, you are fundamentally limited by real-world capacity constraints. If you buy land or lease land for a data center, you are constrained by the size of the land, the utility capacity, and the networking infrastructure – essentially limiting how much hardware you can fit onto that land. If you buy a certain number of servers, you are limited by the constraints of the components of that server, such as the motherboard for the amount of CPUs, RAM, and storage that can be attached to that server.

To maximize the cost-performance ratios of on-premises or private infrastructure, companies typically procure data center hardware and software in bulk. Therefore, they make major commitments that impact their ability to adapt to changes in the market and adopt new technologies. For example, if you sign a contract with a hardware manufacturer to procure a specific type of server today, perhaps a new graphics card is launched in a year or two and the hardware on the server may not be able to support that new hardware. Another example would be to procure licenses in bulk for an operating system that may not be needed if the system or application that is being implemented has different requirements.

Scalability

When scaling an application, there are many things to consider. How do we architect for a global audience? How do we make data accessible to global users without compromising security and regulatory standards? What tools and technologies are optimal for building global systems? Although this can be done via the traditional, on-premises approach, it would take years of planning and development. Meanwhile, with a public cloud provider, you can quickly define and execute a plan, given the abstraction of having to procure and manage the physical infrastructure.

The technology considerations, validation, and implementation can also often be much easier with a public cloud provider. They have existing relationships with vendors, offer their services via a marketplace, and can handle the procurement via their platform. This makes it much easier to get hands-on with technology as everything is one API call away and the vendors tend to build partnerships and integrations with independent software vendors.

Hyperscale cloud providers also offer a myriad of services, typically built on first-party or open source technologies, which provide their customers with a platform upon which to build. Developers and architects can quickly iterate on system design by testing benchmark performance and getting a meaningful understanding of cost. These services can also be autoscaling and fault-tolerant, allowing folks to build systems that scale up to the peak but also scale down during off-peak hours. This enables teams to pay for infrastructure that they use rather than paying for infrastructure, regardless of whether or not it's needed.

Reliability

Reliability is a key metric for applications, particularly when those systems need to be on 24 hours a day, 7 days a week, and every week of the year. An example of an application that needs to be online at all times would be a consumer-facing banking application. It doesn't matter if it's 3 A.M. on a Tuesday or if you're in Europe – you would expect the banking application for your American retail bank to be functional, accessible, and secure, regardless of where you access it from and the time of day. Perhaps you lost your plane ticket and needed to purchase a new one or you ran out of cash and needed to withdraw additional funds. The application being down may not only impact your ability to travel back home but also your ability to procure goods and services you require to live, such as shelter, water, and food. In a world where funds are digital, having the banking application unavailable for any period could be considered unacceptable.

When trying to understand how important reliability is for customers, it's helpful to think about the impact of the application going offline. Depending on the circumstances, your application may have little to no usage outside of business hours or your office. In this circumstance, you may be able to weather a database being offline for several hours as teams patch or upgrade the underlying infrastructure, hardware, operating system, or application. However, for applications that are externally facing and need to serve global users for a business-critical workload – you need as much uptime as possible.

Some common terms around reliability are *four 9s* or *five 9s* of uptime. This refers to the percentage of time services were available over a certain period – typically a year. For example, if your application or service provides *four 9s* of uptime, it would be available 99.99% of the time over a year, translating to about 52 minutes of downtime per year. An even higher bar for uptime is *five 9s*, where your application is available 99.999% of the time over a year – totaling only 6 minutes of downtime.

When working with public cloud, reliability is often one of the reasons cited as justification for the migration. Public cloud providers abstract away much of the physical complexity of managing uptime and ensuring infrastructure is consistently available to users. By leveraging hyperscale platforms, companies can build on top of services that can natively autoscale based on load, have redundancy built in, and are architected across multiple regions or zones. This would be achievable with private cloud but the costs would be enormous. Often, organizations such as banks will run multiple data centers that are essentially replicas of each other to be able to recover from and deal with issues related to major outages. With public cloud, in particular **Google Cloud**, it's very easy to build multiregional infrastructure and architect network traffic failover with multi-regional datastores. This ensures that when a region does go down, your application can still funnel traffic to functional infrastructure and access the data it needs.

Elasticity

The ability to dynamically scale infrastructure based on traffic and needs is another advantage of leveraging public cloud. When running infrastructure on-premises or in a private cloud, you're fundamentally limited by the available physical space for the infrastructure and how much infrastructure you own. Not only is it tough to grow beyond the real-world, physical constraints but whenever you have infrastructure that's not in use – either allocated for peak loads or future capacity – you're paying for hardware to sit on a shelf.

IT teams building or managing infrastructure themselves have to spend a lot of time planning for and building out capacity that is very expensive to procure. These costs pile up as you look at real estate, physical security, warehousing, power, and cooling, and we haven't even gotten to the licensing and hardware costs yet! From there, you need to procure servers and networking equipment, wire it all together, and install all of the relevant software, such as approved operating systems, applications, and security tooling such as antivirus and monitoring software. As you can imagine, this isn't very flexible. If you have a capacity you don't use, you still have to pay for any licensing and other associated costs that may come with that infrastructure.

Assuming you don't have enough capacity, being able to scale up is an even bigger challenge. Being able to forecast hardware utilization, especially as teams are launching new applications or projects, can be challenging. If you have run out of physical space, it may take a few years to onboard a new data center with meaningful capacity. You must often plan months or even years ahead to map out the required hardware capacity to have it available for the team at the right time. Any major world event may impact your ability to deliver on that capacity. We saw this in 2020 and 2022, when supply chains were disrupted, and therefore so was the ability for hardware vendors to make their shipments on time.

Meanwhile, in public cloud, vendors have data centers all over the world, and with the click of a button or the call of an API, you can spin up a new region or request more capacity for a workload. This flexibility allows companies to only pay for the infrastructure that they use, which contrasts with the approach where they must pay for the infrastructure they think they may use 2 years from now. This allows for better cost of ownership and for the IT budget to match or at least correlate with how the business is doing overall. If the business is struggling and has fewer users, infrastructure can easily be scaled down to match the new reality. If there is suddenly a spike in usage that proves to be a longer-term trend, you can easily scale up to meet this demand.

Agility

To compete in the fast-paced technology market of today, companies are focused on ensuring that they can maximize the productivity of their developers and teams. Engineering teams are very expensive from a headcount standpoint. Therefore, by maximizing the utilization and productivity of their engineer, an organization can ensure that they are matching or beating their competitors when it comes to building and launching features, products, and services.

With a private cloud environment, developers constantly run into technical blockers when trying to build, test, and launch code. Between requests for provisioning development environments, building and automating tests, and pushing to production, it can be very painful when developers have to work with other teams to get access to critical tools and systems.

Developers working on public cloud have the benefit of being significantly more agile given that they don't have to run into physical restraints on building new environments for development, testing, and production deployments. With the click of a button or a set of API calls, a developer can quickly and easily spin up infrastructure, segment it out into *development*, *test*, and *production* environments, and execute on their job. This feeds well into the practice of **Agile** software development as it makes it easier and faster for technology teams to collaborate and maximize productivity.

Cost

Cost is also a significant factor that drives the adoption of public cloud environments. The amount of capital investment to get a physical, self-hosted, and managed environment off the ground is massive. Often, you have to procure capacity for potential future usage, and organizations are forced to spend millions of dollars on all the associated costs of building and running their data centers.

Between buying or leasing land, standing up, or renting a structure that meets the data center requirements, power, cooling, and headcount – these projects can take years to get off the ground and require massive capital expenditure.

In contrast, public cloud providers offer pay-as-you-go services that allow you to pay purely for the infrastructure that you use and some even provide tooling to help optimize the environment based on historical usage patterns. This helps organizations right-size their infrastructure and only pay for the capacity that they need rather than paying for hardware to sit on a shelf in the hopes that it may be needed someday.

The additional burden of having to harden and secure both the physical and digital components of the data center requires mature security teams, practices, and technologies – all of which increase the cost burden of building, running, and managing your infrastructure.

In summary, there are many factors why an organization would adopt public cloud. Whether they're a fledgling startup that wants to build a global gaming company or a large regional bank that is looking to better serve clients in a digital age, the benefits, such as scalability, flexibility, reliability, agility, and cost, make a strong argument for adopting public cloud environments.

The impact of cloud adoption on finance teams

Beyond reducing the amount of planning and capital required to build and operate technology companies, the shift from large capital expenditures to a consumption-based expenditure model also represents a big shift in how companies and finance departments think about technology costs.

Building and running private cloud environments is very costly. It requires massive amounts of capital and significant time to activate that capital. Therefore, over the past couple of decades, finance departments have understood that when it comes to procuring technology, you should expect large deal sizes and for the capital to be spent upfront. This meant that checks needed to be sent to all the different vendors to buy the different components of the data center before the data center would come online. There would be months if not years of lead time between when a company was able to purchase something and when they were able to use it.

Given this large lead time from procurement to delivery, finance teams were ready for multi-year contracts with large contract sizes, which would allow them to buy hardware and software in bulk – minimizing cost while maximizing capacity. If they only needed 20 servers for the next couple of months or years, they might have pushed for the procurement of 30 to 40 servers to ensure the company could continue to grow for the next 3 to 5 years before the hardware becomes obsolete and needs to be refreshed. Similarly, to match the hardware procurement cycle and build more predictability into the business, software procurement followed a similar route. Vendors would push customers to sign contracts to buy software licenses upfront for several years, allowing them to provide the customer with a meaningful discount and lock them in for a few years.

Although these concepts continue to exist, even in the public cloud space, there has been a shift in mentality when it comes to procuring and delivering technology. Hyperscale cloud providers can be more creative with pricing across the different services that they offer, given that they can procure hardware and software at a scale that most companies would never reach. Rather than discussing petabytes of data, hyperscale providers have exabytes of capacity. Similarly, rather than procuring hundreds or thousands of servers and their components, they can justify the procurement of hundreds of thousands – if not millions – of servers and components at a time. This allows them to be more creative and flexible with pricing for their customers as they can realize significant savings from the hardware and software manufacturers when they procure in bulk.

With the advent of cloud computing, hyperscaler providers, public cloud, and auto-scaling infrastructure, we've seen the rise of a consumption-based model of paying for technology. Rather than paying upfront for years' worth of hardware and software, technology teams benefit from a pay-as-you-go model where they only pay for the infrastructure that they use. They can also architect systems that can scale up and down based on demand, minimizing the impact of having to pay for idle infrastructure.

Assuming a company does reach a point where they want to outline commercial terms for a commitment to consume a public cloud platform at a lower cost, those mechanisms are still in place and they can still go through the traditional contracting flow. The main difference with Google Cloud, for example, is that customers aren't required to pay the value of the contract upfront. Even if they do outline a 3-year contract, the contract will be paid down based on their actual consumption. You may commit to spending $100,000 over 3 years but instead of paying that cost upfront in bulk, companies only pay for the infrastructure that they consume every month.

This shift from upfront payment to monthly payment is important as it shifts the classification of certain costs for accounting and finance departments. If something is a large cost and is paid in bulk at one point in time, it is considered a **capital expenditure**. When something is paid for on an ongoing basis, typically broken down into recurring payments based on a specific window of time – monthly, for example–it's considered an **operating expenditure**.

Depending on the classification of a payment, there may be different processes and budgets to pull from; therefore, it's important to be aware that the shift to public cloud not only impacts technology teams or executives but also touches other meaningful departments, such as finance and legal teams. This also means that the cost burden of getting a technology company off the ground has lessened considerably. No longer does it take a large, global team of engineers to build out a company's infrastructure to serve clients across the globe. All you need is a browser and an internet connection and you can spin up infrastructure almost anywhere in the world where the public cloud providers have data centers.

It's important to keep in mind that all of the preceding implications mean that the **total cost of ownership** (**TCO**) of cloud environments can often end up being less – even if you end up having to pay a bit more for modern technologies. When you factor in the total cost of building, managing, and operating your infrastructure, it means millions of dollars across real estate, power, and people costs. From there, you also need to ensure your infrastructure is reliable and secure, which requires even more investment. By abstracting away the physical components of technology infrastructure and empowering organizations to do it all virtually, over the internet, public cloud providers take on much of the cost burdens associated with maintaining those kinds of environments while passing on the benefits of procuring and building data centers on a global scale.

Private, public, or hybrid?

Now that we've explored the benefits and challenges related to private and public cloud environments, let's discuss when each of those environments makes sense or when you may use both! The term **hybrid cloud** refers to an organization that leverages both private and public cloud environments. It is quite common to find organizations that are running hybrid cloud environments when they've been around for a while and have already made significant investments in building out their data centers. Rather than completely discounting historical investments, organizations may choose to slowly sunset their existing data centers based on existing contractual and hardware life cycle constraints. For example, if they refreshed all of the hardware in one of their data centers a year ago and the hardware still has 4 years before it becomes obsolete, that company may choose to migrate infrastructure from other data centers to the public cloud while retaining the recently refreshed data center. This may mean that they need to extend their private cloud environment to the public cloud and allow the two environments to cooperate, essentially building a hybrid environment where they both own and manage their own data centers while also leveraging a public cloud environment.

Regarding when one environment makes more sense than the other, you typically see organizations leveraging private clouds exclusively when they need to maintain strict control over their data and applications, have regulatory requirements that they need to meet, or want to avoid vendor lock-in. An example of this could be an organization in the aerospace industry that works with government contracts. If they want to be vendor-agnostic and meet very stringent compliance requirements, such as **FedRAMP High**, it may make sense for them to build and manage their infrastructure. (You can learn more about FedRAMP compliance here: `https://www.fedramp.gov/understanding-baselines-and-impact-levels/`.)

By contrast, organizations that serve external applications globally or need to be able to dynamically scale infrastructure up and down would find public cloud environments to be more appropriate to address their needs. Teams that want to benefit from the latest advances in technology may also find public cloud environments to be optimal given that hyperscale providers often build and launch either proprietary or open source technologies as a managed service, allowing them to quickly test, validate, launch, and iterate on these services.

In large organizations, it is quite common to have both public and private cloud environments as different business units and applications have different needs. If you have a specialized, internal quoting tool for US government contracts, it may make sense to keep that system in a private data center – especially if you've already obtained all the appropriate certifications. Meanwhile, if one of the other divisions is focused on a consumer product that uses little to no sensitive data and needs to be able to handle large variations in traffic across the globe, a public cloud environment would likely be ideal.

Now that we have a better understanding of where public, private, and hybrid cloud environments make sense, let's dig deeper into what makes Google Cloud different from other public cloud providers. But part of the magic of Google Cloud, making it unique relative to other public cloud providers, is the fact that the platform was built on top of Google's existing networking infrastructure. To truly understand why this point of differentiation is so important, we need to understand why networking is important.

An introduction to networks

In this section, we'll dig into networking basics such as terminology and architecture.

An **IP address** is a unique identifier that is assigned to any machine that is connecting to a network. This identifier helps ensure that traffic is routed correctly. For example, when you send a request to `google.com`, the web page needs to know who made that request to provide the answer to the correct machine. You can think of an IP address as a home address for your laptop, mobile device, or server. It designates where the request is coming from and where the response needs to go.

Every machine connected to the internet has an IP address, including web servers hosting websites. What we type into a browser and understand to be the domain of the website (`www.google.com`) is not used by machines to understand the destination. Rather, these human-legible names for sites get converted into IP addresses for the machine to understand where the request is coming from and where it needs to go. A **domain name service** (**DNS**) is a system that translates domain names into IP addresses. They take the input from your browser and look up the appropriate IP address for the request. Once that has been identified, they send the data to the appropriate destination so that the request is resolved.

The website request, after being translated into an IP address, will go from your home or office to an **internet service provider** (**ISP**), which will then route the traffic to the destination. ISPs are essentially the backbone of what we call the internet – they are a series of globally distributed companies that have built out a network of high-speed **fiber optic cables** to serve their clients. The internet is essentially a web of distributed networks, owned and managed by these ISPs. Fiber optic cables use light to transmit information, making it extremely fast and less susceptible to interference relative to copper cables. Between large, regional ISPs, some of which may be an ocean apart, you'll find **subsea cables** connecting them to form the global internet we think of today. To get internet traffic from North America to Europe, Africa, or Asia, you must first build the networking infrastructure across the Atlantic or Pacific oceans. Depending on the circumstances, the destination may be Google's major data centers or a **network edge data center**. Infrastructure at the edge of the network is quite common when content needs to be delivered with low latency. The edge refers to infrastructure that brings computing and data as close to the end user as possible. This allows better response times and therefore performance relative to centralized, data center infrastructure. If you work at a sports stadium, this may mean hosting infrastructure at the stadium that can process the sports video feed in real time to generate highlights and snapshots.

Latency is typically measured in milliseconds and is essentially the measure of how long it takes for data to travel from one point to another. If you want to watch the latest TV show that is very popular on your favorite streaming platform, that platform is likely hosting that content in an edge location to improve your experience. Video and image files for example are very large files and can take a long time to transmit from the centralized data center to the end user. By storing some commonly used data at the edge, such as a very popular TV show, a streaming platform would be able to avoid connectivity or latency issues with its content and provide a better consumer experience. They would also save on the cost related to transmitting the data from the central repository of content to the end user by routing that traffic to the edge location. Another common term related to networking performance is bandwidth. **Bandwidth** refers to how much traffic or data can be transferred over a network within a window of time. It is measured in **bits per second** (**BPS**) and designates the volume of data that can be transmitted via a specific cable or network. For example, applications that stream content such as high-quality videos may require a connection with at least 3 GB per hour in bandwidth per person, while a gaming application may require 100 MB per hour per person.

Now that we have a better understanding of how networks function as a whole, let's explore how Google's proprietary global network impacts Google Cloud.

Public cloud with Google Cloud

Google has built a global network of data centers that is connected by proprietary cables and networks. This means that although Google may work with or partner with ISPs in certain cases, all traffic traveling over the Google network is traveling outside of the public internet. This is unique to Google as it is the only hyperscale cloud provider to have built out this global network. The reason for this infrastructure is that to support the expectations of users for Google Search to be lightning fast, Google engineers decided to build their own global, private network. This prevents them from being at the mercy of latency, bandwidth, or security issues related to working with regional ISPs and ensures that they will have the networking capacity required to support future growth – even if local ISPs don't meet Google's technical requirements. The following figure highlights Google's global network across the existing network, subsea cable investments, and where Google has edge points of presence:

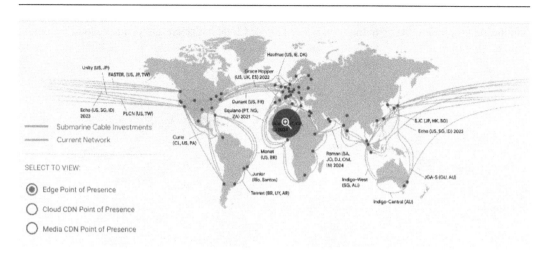

Figure 2.1 – Google's global network at a glance (source: https://cloud.
google.com/about/locations#lightbox-regions-map)

Google Cloud's data centers are broken down into different regions to designate major data centers and each region is segmented into zones. Most regions will have at least three **zones**, with each zone isolated from the other, having its own dedicated power and cooling mechanisms, allowing you to build redundancy within regions. By having separate zones within regions, Google can virtually isolate these zones from each other, which reduces the risk of all of the infrastructure going offline for the region in which the customer is building. For example, a customer may architect a system to have replicas or disaster recovery capabilities from one zone to the other, increasing the reliability of its systems and reducing the probability that a major outage will take all of the systems in that region offline.

The following figure identifies all of the cities where Google Cloud has active and planned cloud regions:

Figure 2.2 – Google Cloud global data center region locations (source: https://cloud.google.com/about/locations#lightbox-regions-map)

Each region within Google Cloud will have at least three availability zones. Some regions may have as many as four zones. The following figure highlights Google Cloud's total network presence from regions to zones, network edge locations, and countries where the network is available:

Figure 2.3 – Networking overview – regions, zones, edge, and countries

What's unique about having a cloud platform built on top of Google's infrastructure is that Google essentially has one global cloud platform. All of the Google data centers are accessible via one cloud console and communication over the Google network infrastructure is encrypted by default both at rest and in transit. This means that if you're looking to build a global company or architect for multiple regions, it can all be done with one console and with minimal configuration. Google Cloud also abstracts away having to manage much of the physical networking infrastructure that you would typically find in a normal data center. Google Cloud has global, software-defined networking capabilities, allowing you to spin up servers on five continents and have them communicating securely in minutes. In contrast, other hyperscale cloud providers operate their different data centers as standalone data centers that are not natively interconnected. If you want to build infrastructure across multiple regions, you need to access each region separately, stand up the environment from scratch, and weave them together to communicate securely via a VPN tunnel, for example. In Google Cloud, you have global connectivity for all regions and zones out of the box, with the traffic being encrypted at rest and in transit by default.

Another implication of having a global network and software-defined networking is that Google Cloud environments can be architected with multi-regional services and dynamically route traffic based on capacity and scalability. For example, you could implement a system that has data stores distributed over multiple regions and if one of the regions fails, that traffic can be routed to the next closest region so that the technical team can resolve the issue with the end user being minimally impacted by the outage.

By having control over its global network, Google Cloud helps customers overcome challenges related to cloud computing, bandwidth, and latency. Customers can often experience equal to or better performance for their applications given that the traffic is going over Google's global, private network. Users and employees around the world can often notice a noticeable difference between the experience of using an application running on Google Cloud versus an application running on-premises or on another cloud provider. If networking performance matters for the experience of an application, the Google network can have a big impact on improving that experience. That's why many gaming companies, such as Niantic, have chosen to work with Google Cloud, even for major launches such as **Pokémon Go**. You can read more about Niantic using Google Cloud here: `https://cloud.google.com/blog/topics/developers-practitioners/how-pok%C3%A9mon-go-scales-millions-requests`.

Google's network equips its clients with unique advantages relative to its competitors. Traffic flowing over the Google network will be more secure, reliable, and performant relative to folks who try to build their own data centers and networking infrastructure.

Summary

The shift from private to public cloud was catalyzed by the needs of employees and customers. Whether it's teams looking to be more productive or customers asking for better availability or new features, the public cloud is a great way to build infrastructure that's highly secure, available, reliable, and performant. While the same technical benefits may be achieved or nearly replicated in private cloud environments, organizations would be hard-pressed to deliver the same quality of service at the same cost relative to public cloud.

Building data centers is no small feat and entire teams would be required for the planning and management of the physical components of the infrastructure. By specializing their engineering teams and focusing on building performant code and new features, companies can out-innovate their competition.

Understanding the shift to public cloud as well as networks as a whole provides us with the foundational knowledge upon which to expand as we delve deeper into the world of the cloud. In *Chapter 3*, we'll dig into the different hosting models that cloud providers have developed over the years as they drove their customers to adopt their solutions and adapted based on different needs.

Understanding the Different Cloud Computing Models

The term **cloud** is often used to refer to or describe a myriad of different hosting models ranging from **Infrastructure-as-a-Service (IaaS)**, through **Platform-as-a-Service (PaaS)**, to **Software-as-a-Service (SaaS)**. While SaaS models have been around for a while and many consumers and business people are familiar with this concept, once you start going deeper into the stack and differentiating between infrastructure and platform services, things often become more difficult to understand given the technical complexity of the topics.

In this chapter, we'll be introducing the concept of the **shared responsibility model** for cloud infrastructure and exploring how it relates to technical decision-making for technology architecture.

By the end of this chapter, you will be able to do the following:

- Define SaaS, PaaS, and IaaS
- Compare and contrast the different hosting models as they relate to the following:
  - Total cost of ownership
  - Flexibility
  - Shared responsibilities
  - Management level
  - Staffing and expertise
- Determine which model is appropriate in different scenarios and use cases
- Describe the shared responsibility model and what falls under the purview of the hosting provider versus the customer relative to on-premises environments

This chapter covers the following topics:

- Introducing cloud hosting models and the shared responsibility model

- Comparing and contrasting IaaS, PaaS, and SaaS

- Going beyond Iaas, Paas, and SaaS

Introducing cloud hosting models and the shared responsibility model

When an organization hosts its infrastructure, they are responsible for all of the different components that come together to deliver the services required by its business. They procure and string together hardware components such as servers and networking equipment, and they implement the virtualization layer for their infrastructure. They also select and manage which operating systems will be leveraged for their applications, manage the runtime environment, manage the scaling of the infrastructure as load increases, launch and manage the application, and finally upload and manage the associated data.

As you can imagine, this is a lot for technology teams to oversee. It can require months of planning to deliver new infrastructure across capacity planning, procurement, logistics, implementation, optimization, hardening, and monitoring. The heavy human and capital expenditure required to self-host created much of the pain that eventually birthed the cloud computing model. Even software vendors would go through considerable pain when helping customers implement their technologies. They were at the mercy of the current state of the customer environment and whatever hardware requirements existed. This may have meant that a software sales cycle would be delayed for weeks or months specifically because you depended on customers to receive your hardware, rack it, connect it to their network, and make it available for use. Problems could go wrong for so many different reasons: a network cable being nonfunctional, hardware or software incompatibility, or even improper implementation. New words began to evolve from these experiences, such as **shelfware**, which is software that you buy but never actually implement to a point where you are deriving the value that was intended from an application.

The SaaS revolution completely changed how organizations and their teams were able to use applications. Rather than having to rely on their infrastructure and teams to serve an application from inside their private cloud, they were able to access an application through the internet. This had a profound impact on how accessible technology became within organizations as they were able to cast off the shackles of complex internal processes and easily leverage new technology. Software providers also benefited greatly from this approach given that they were able to get their technology directly in the hands of end users across the globe without first having to navigate physical procurement challenges.

Examples of SaaS technologies from the Google Cloud ecosystem are Gmail, Google Docs, and Google Drive. Gmail is an email hosting service and one of the core components of Google Workspace, Google's Enterprise productivity suite. Google Docs is a cloud-native document editor that leverages the strengths of the SaaS model by having documents accessible over the internet and multiple people to collaborate on them simultaneously. Google Drive is a web-based cloud data repository where users can upload any file type, such as documents, image files, or spreadsheets, to easily work on and access them if needed. These solutions or variations of them have often been the first exposure most people have to the cloud. These solutions also created new ways of working, where documents weren't locked down to physical machines or hard drives and were accessible over the internet, all around the world. Folks were able to collaborate at a scale and speed that previously wouldn't be possible.

Naturally, with this newfound freedom came risk. Organizations were willing to trade the control of the infrastructure for the benefits of agility or innovation, but they needed cloud vendors to take ownership of securing the infrastructure on which the application was hosted. Some organizations found themselves in industries where data security was of utmost importance. They may have been banks, hospitals, or government organizations that were held accountable to national or even global regulatory standards. To ensure that these organizations would maintain compliance with these stringent requirements and be comfortable procuring externally hosted software, the **shared responsibility model** was developed. This model outlines what components of the infrastructure the hosting provider would be responsible for and which components the client was responsible for. This helped legal and regulatory teams understand who should be held accountable relative to data breaches and therefore define a legal and contractual framework for this new technology model. Technical teams also adapted as the needs became more specialized, with concepts such as **SRE** and **developer operations** becoming more widespread.

The development of IaaS and accessing infrastructure over the internet was also very significant for technology teams. Cloud providers began to offer virtualization as a service, where they would provide the physical infrastructure components of a data center over the internet as a service. Their clients would still be able to interact with the environment and manage it from a server design and operation system level but all of the physical, real-world complexities were abstracted away. If you needed a new server of a specific size in a specific location, the configuration and deployment of that server were now a few clicks away. Much of the pain and stress from managing your infrastructure comes from all the potential points of failure across the technology stack. Whenever an application goes offline at peak demand, there are many reasons as to why that might happen. There may have been a networking failure, whether it was caused by a misconfiguration, a recent patch, or a cable issue. Perhaps the code base was the problem, or not enough hardware was provisioned to handle the load.

While these issues still exist when using cloud providers, the organization can trust that the cloud provider will have specific capabilities for managing the physical components of the infrastructure. One of the big benefits of leveraging public cloud is that outages are publicly reported, which creates a culture of accountability while also incentivizing global downtime minimization. While organizations shouldn't rely exclusively on these providers and still build fault tolerance into their infrastructure, this significantly reduces the cost and complexity of managing technology infrastructure. Another benefit is that the regulatory frameworks specific to the physical components of the infrastructure apply to the cloud provider and therefore propagate to their customers. IaaS cloud customers are still responsible for configuring the infrastructure platform itself and therefore oversee the virtualized infrastructure across **identity and access management** (**IAM**), operating systems (selection, versioning, and management), the configurations and provisioning of **virtual machines** (**VMs**), their associated applications and the data in those applications.

The Google Cloud IaaS service is referred to as **Compute Engine**. Compute Engine allows customers to spin up VMs and manage applications in the same way that they would through a virtualization service. Technology teams can select the machine's size, either through one of the pre-selected configurations or even build their own, custom VM, and select which operating system to use. From there, they install applications on those systems, connect them to a network, and make them available for others to access, similar to other virtualization services. They are also responsible for network configuration, monitoring, and other components. Google Cloud also provides additional value with **Managed Instance Groups** (**MIGs**). MIGs allow you to make VM-based infrastructure more reliable and scalable through automation by offering services such as autoscaling, autohealing, distributed deployments, and automatic updates. This can be very valuable for organizations that experience inconsistent traffic patterns for their applications. A gaming company, for example, can leverage MIGs to dynamically scale their infrastructure and ensure that they can handle large influxes of gamers without the backend infrastructure collapsing. It also optimizes for cost given that instance groups can also scale down assuming traffic tapers off. (You can read more here: `https://cloud.google.com/compute/docs/instance-groups`.)

In addition to SaaS and IaaS hosting models, there is also the PaaS model. PaaS solutions provide value to technology teams by abstracting away the need to manage infrastructure while allowing them to develop, host, and manage applications. This enables teams to invest less in infrastructure-focused technical headcount and more in development headcount, empowering them to build more code faster. If an organization's core business is in software and application development, such tools are very powerful in helping them focus resources on building new features and delivering on product roadmaps. This focus allows them to maintain pace with and even out-innovate competitors who are less efficient with their headcount and resource allocation.

Examples of Google Cloud's PaaS services are App Engine and the Vertex AI platform. App Engine is an application hosting and management platform that allows developers to deploy code while completely abstracting away much of the infrastructure management. There is no need to build, launch, and manage VMs and operating systems. Developers simply deploy code and press launch. App Engine dynamically spins up infrastructure on the backend to handle the demand on the infrastructure and can scale it up and down based on the traffic. An example of a company using App Engine to scale quickly is Snap. When originally launching **Snapchat**, the social media sensation of the 2010s, the application had a monolithic architecture and was deployed on App Engine. According to the Snap engineering blog (you can read it at `https://eng.snap.com/monolith-to-multicloud-microservices-snap-service-mesh`), the benefit of App Engine was that it was able to accommodate rapid growth in features, engineers, and customers.

The Vertex AI platform provides a development environment for data and ML teams to build, test, validate, launch, catalog, and iterate on ML models with ease. It's built on top of Google's recently launched practice of **machine learning operations** (**MLOps**), which outlines best practices for full life cycle model management. Some of the highlights of the platform are Vertex AI Workbench, a managed Jupyter notebook environment with pre-installed packages and integrations; Vertex AI Pipelines, which helps with ML workflow orchestration through serverless services; and Model Garden, a catalog of ML models provided by Google and its partners that can be used to kickstart ML projects. The head of ad tech for Wayfair, for example, highlights how the Vertex AI platform and the MLOps approach to ML reduces time to value for AI models for his company (you can read it here: `https://www. forbes.com/sites/googlecloud/2021/11/29/3-steps-to-scale-ml-models- and-drive-more-business-impact/?sh=47a3f8693431`):

> *"We're doing ML at a massive scale, and we want to make that easy. That means accelerating time-to-value for new models, increasing the reliability and speed of very large regular re-training jobs, and reducing the friction to build and deploy models at scale… Certain large model training jobs are 5-10x faster with Vertex AI, and it offers our data scientists hyperparameter tuning. This enables us to weave ML into the fabric of how we make decisions."*

In summary, the shared responsibility model outlines the different layers of technology infrastructure and who is responsible for the different components, depending on the type of solution. In the next section, we'll dive deeper into the core hosting models to compare and contrast them.

Comparing and contrasting IaaS, PaaS, and SaaS

To prepare for the Cloud Digital Leader exam, you must have a firm understanding of the differences between the different hosting environments and their tradeoffs. We'll be diving deeper into the models across the following variables: **total cost of ownership** (**TCO**), flexibility, shared responsibilities, operational level, and staffing and expertise.

We'll start by digging into the three core models: IaaS, PaaS, and SaaS. From there, we'll touch on **Containers-as-a-Service** (**CaaS**) and **Function-as-a-Service** (**FaaS**), as highlighted by the following breakdown:

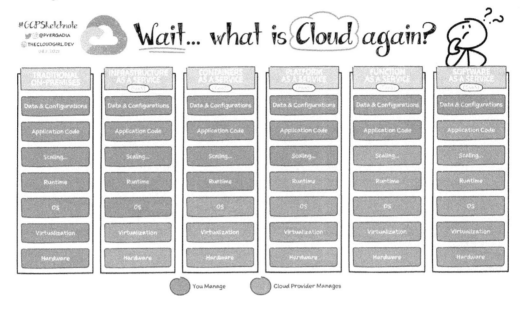

Figure 3.1 — Client versus cloud provider responsibility matrix
(source: https://cloud.google.com/learn/paas-vs-iaas-vs-saas)

Let's check them out.

IaaS

IaaS is a cloud computing service model that delivers on-demand infrastructure resources to organizations via the cloud, such as compute, storage, networking, and virtualization. Customers don't have to manage, maintain, or update their own data center infrastructure, but they are responsible for the operating system, middleware, VMs, and any apps or data.

Let's check out the variables for IaaS.

Total cost of ownership (TCO)

From a technology perspective, IaaS environments may be more cost-efficient from a hardware and infrastructure perspective but often, when you take into consideration the TCO across licensing and headcount, among other factors, it has the highest total cost. An organization that migrates from on-premises environments to an IaaS provider may not adopt architecture best practices for cloud environments and therefore bring much of the cost burdens of the on-premises assets with them to the cloud.

This often includes existing contracts and licensing with software manufacturers for operating systems, databases, and more. This approach still has several benefits as it shifts the large capital expenditures of managing a data center to operating expenditures, offloads security and compliance responsibilities to the cloud provider, and empowers teams to quickly provision infrastructure.

Flexibility

IaaS is the most flexible model out of the three core cloud computing models. Infrastructure teams have complete control over the infrastructure above the virtualization layer. They can select machine types, even the types and amount of cores that may be assigned to a VM, giving them granular control over the servers that will be running their applications. This also means that they are less restricted by the platform relative to the other models. However, there are still some limitations – for example, other cloud providers may force you into certain pre-built machine types based on what they've procured and what capacity is available. Google offers pre-configured machine types but customers are also free to define their own, custom machine sizes to maximize cost-to-performance ratios.

Shared responsibilities

Within the IaaS model, the cloud provider is specifically responsible for the hardware and virtualization layer of the infrastructure. They procure server and networking hardware, manage the land, cooling, and power associated with the hardware, and are also responsible for the physical security of the location. They make their infrastructure available through virtualization over the internet, allowing clients to spin up VMs on their infrastructure.

Meanwhile, the IaaS customer is responsible for everything above the virtualization layer. Let's break this down very clearly:

- IaaS vendor responsibilities:

  - Hardware

  - Virtualization

- IaaS customer responsibilities:

  - Operating system

  - Runtime

  - Scaling

  - Application

  - Data and configuration

Management level

IaaS environments are the most involved from a management perspective given that technology teams directly oversee and control significant portions of the technology stack. They are responsible for securing the data in that environment and also need to implement disaster recovery and fault tolerance into their systems. This often includes tasks such as managing database backups, running parallel **hot-hot** or **hot-cold** environments as a means of reducing the risk of critical failures, and minimizing the impact breaches or outages.

Hot-hot refers to having multiple, redundant data centers that can pick up the traffic for another should one of them fail. In a hot-cold environment, you have a primary data center that hosts production workloads while your backup cold data center is used mainly for storage and archival. Effectively, it's not a replica of the hot data center nor intended to handle production traffic.

Staffing and expertise

Organizations leveraging IaaS services require a specific set of skills not only across the cloud platform itself but also across all of the systems and applications being used to host the applications. This means that team members will need to have exposure and familiarity with managing VMs and operating systems. Although this is a common skill set, it doesn't provide a lot of value to the organization other than maintaining operations. Teams will often hire database administrators and infrastructure or virtualization experts and spend a significant amount of time micromanaging and overseeing the infrastructure. They've essentially shifted the on-premises working model to a cloud environment and retained the need for many of the skills associated with those environments.

IaaS offerings can essentially be thought of as virtualization as a service, where the cloud provider is responsible for the virtualization layer itself and everything else underneath that layer of infrastructure while the client is responsible for everything above that layer. It includes spinning up VMs and sizing them, as well as installing operating systems and patching them. The shift to PaaS abstracts away some of that fine-grained control over infrastructure to simplify the usage of developer tools and applications.

PaaS

PaaS is a cloud computing service model that delivers and manages all the hardware and software resources to develop applications through the cloud. Developers and IT operations teams can use PaaS to develop, run, and manage applications without having to build and maintain the infrastructure or platform on their own. Customers still have to write the code and manage their data and applications, but the environment to build and deploy apps is managed and maintained by the cloud service provider. Let's check out the variables for PaaS.

TCO

PaaS customers might feel like their cloud bills are more expensive than if they were running their infrastructure but this is typically not the case when you look at it from a TCO perspective. Although they might spend more on technology, they no longer have to spend a significant amount of money and headcount on managing the infrastructure itself. Teams leveraging PaaS solutions no longer need to pay for the cost and management of the underlying infrastructure, allowing them to avoid large, multi-year licensing contracts for operating systems, for example as PaaS platforms have abstracted it away. PaaS solutions have a lower TCO than IaaS solutions but higher than SaaS solutions.

Flexibility

Teams building on top of PaaS technologies will find themselves more restricted than when using IaaS cloud solutions. Because they don't manage the underlying infrastructure of the platforms, they won't be able to freely choose and adapt those components. Platforms will be restricted to what the cloud provider can support through their technology. Examples of this are that specific PaaS hosting platforms may only support specific runtime environments, programming languages, or versions of programming languages. Support of new releases for a specific programming language, for example, may take some time to translate to a production-grade release by the PaaS provider.

Shared responsibilities

When offering PaaS solutions to clients, the cloud provider is responsible for the hardware, virtualization layer, operating systems, and runtime environment. Everything above those layers is the responsibility of the PaaS client. This includes scaling the platform, the application code running in the environment, the data, and the associated configuration. Let's break this down, similar to the previous subsection:

- PaaS vendor responsibilities:

  - Hardware

  - Virtualization

  - Operating system

  - Runtime

- PaaS customer responsibilities:

  - Scaling

  - Application

  - Data and configuration

Management level

PaaS environments require significantly less time and resources to manage relative to IaaS environments. Much of the technical complexity of configuring and managing infrastructure is abstracted away so that data and development teams can focus on deriving value from the platform rather than keeping the platform running, secure, and reliable. There are still components that need to be managed, such as scaling, but this is often relatively easy to do through the platform, and new capabilities are typically offered, such as canary deployments and traffic splitting with App Engine (`https://cloud.google.com/appengine/docs/legacy/standard/python/splitting-traffic`). **Traffic splitting** is where you deploy a new version of the application and only funnel a percentage of the traffic to the new version to validate that there are no issues that may cause an outage. Building out this sort of production testing infrastructure and managing the traffic from an IaaS perspective would take much more time and effort, while with PaaS solutions, it can be achieved with a few clicks of a button.

Staffing and expertise

Teams that choose to leverage PaaS solutions are empowered to specialize their teams around things such as development, data science, and ML. Rather than having folks split expertise across infrastructure and development or data engineering and data science, they abstract away management of the infrastructure and focus them on revenue-generating activities. These teams focus on developing skills that are focused more on enabling the business to move faster and maximizing productivity, which is a very different mentality relative to the traditional, IaaS approach to infrastructure.

Now that we have a better understanding of the PaaS model, let's shift even more to the right in the shared responsibility model as we abstract away infrastructure management to focus more on the application itself. SaaS solutions are typically geared toward end users, with administrators living within the application itself and managing the data in the application exclusively, as well as those who have access to the data and permission to execute specific workflows within the application.

SaaS

SaaS is a cloud computing service model that provides the entire application stack, delivering an entire cloud-based application that customers can access and use. SaaS products are completely managed by the service provider and come ready to use, including all updates, bug fixes, and overall maintenance. Most SaaS applications are accessed directly through a web browser, which means customers don't have to download or install anything on their devices.

Let's check out the variables for SaaS.

TCO

The TCO for SaaS solutions is regarded as the lowest of the different cloud hosting models. Although it may seem more expensive at face value given the licensing cost associated with these solutions, when you take into account the amount of time and effort in building, launching, and maintaining the infrastructure for hosting those systems, the costs are relatively low. SaaS applications tend to be business-facing or consumer-facing and may have significant fluctuations in traffic over time.

Flexibility

The SaaS model is the least flexible of all the cloud models. Given that the provider is delivering an application directly to the end user, you are restricted by that application's dependencies, code, and capabilities. You are essentially forced to adopt the limits of the application and its underlying infrastructure; you have no control over it or its security controls. There is typically minimal customization of the application, if at all possible, and issues around integration with existing tools and systems can become an issue. That being said, it's very easy to use and get started, so there are many benefits to using SaaS systems as well.

Shared responsibilities

Within the shared responsibility model, the SaaS provider is responsible for the entire technology stack from the underlying hardware, up to and including the application code. Clients are responsible for setting up the system and managing the data within the system but the rest is abstracted away. Again, for the sake of simplicity and clarity, let's review the breakdown:

- SaaS vendor responsibilities:

  - Hardware

  - Virtualization

  - Operating system

  - Runtime

  - Scaling

  - Application

- SaaS customer responsibilities:

  - Data and configuration

Management level

From a management perspective, the SaaS provider delivers an application over the internet to your end users and the only control you have over the environment as a client is the data that you upload to it and how the system is configured. Things such as infrastructure optimization, scaling, and managing the application code are abstracted away as the systems are designed for business use. The tradeoff is that users will be limited by the functionality of the system and won't have direct control or influence over the application itself. Any changes to infrastructure or new features must go through the SaaS provider as they will be the ones managing the underlying components of the technology stack.

Staffing and expertise

Technology teams that can leverage SaaS solutions for their business can specialize in system engineers. Given that they no longer need to focus specifically on managing infrastructure or development, they focus on being experts in the systems they implement to ensure they are properly configured and driving the value that the business expects. Examples of this are folks who become **customer relationship management** (**CRM**) system administrators or Google Workspace administrators. They develop skills around how to implement, manage, and secure the system based on its configurations.

While IaaS, PaaS, and SaaS are all common hosting models, depending on the application that you are using, new models for hosting technology in the cloud have also been developed. Providers are exploring different levels of abstraction to where customers may need more control of the environment than in a PaaS environment but not as much control as in an IaaS environment. Similarly, perhaps you need more control over an application than in a SaaS solution but not as much as you would have with a PaaS environment. Let's explore additional variations of the shared responsibility model.

Going beyond IaaS, PaaS, and SaaS

Although it is not specifically called out in the exam preparation guide, it's also helpful to dig into additional variations of the cloud hosting model. As Google Cloud and other cloud providers matured and began to offer more or less flexibility for their technology based on customer needs, they began to launch services that fill the gaps between IaaS, PaaS, and SaaS.

As we dig into Google's hosting services, we'll begin to learn about CaaS and FaaS. Containers and functions are ways to package code to make it run with less cost, time, or effort. The chart from the Google Cloud documentation (featured earlier in *Figure 3.1*) helps articulate the levels of abstraction for these other specialized hosting models as they relate to the shared responsibility model.

Given the focus of this book is to prepare you for the Google Cloud Digital Leader exam, providing some additional context around CaaS and FaaS will help establish the foundational knowledge required to understand why the variations exist.

Containers and CaaS

Containers are an approach to virtualization where you consolidate everything you need to run an application into an executable software package. This includes the code, runtime, system tools, system libraries, and configurations. An important thing to note is because containers share the operating system with their host machine, they are very lightweight, resource-efficient, and portable. This stands in contrast to VMs since they emulate physical machines and therefore each VM requires an operating system.

Containers also pair well with service or microservice-based applications. In the world of on-premises environments and physical machines, an application was built with what was called **monolithic architecture**. This meant that application code was written like a novel, with all of the different components woven together to deliver a set of features and capabilities. This approach to building systems and applications can create issues around scalability, availability, and cost. Because monolithic applications are one large code base, they would also require a significant amount of hardware to be provisioned to a server for it to run and perform.

This approach can inhibit innovation by reducing the release velocity of development teams, given that making changes to a large code base can have unintended consequences and downstream impacts on the code. Changes are very scary to make and can have significant implications on revenue.

By contrast, when you take a service- or microservice-based approach to application development, you break an application down into smaller, more manageable, and independent components. This makes it significantly less risky to launch new features and capabilities given that the different components aren't woven together.

These smaller bits of code that are independent of each other still need to work together to provide a holistic experience to clients. These bits of code are packaged in containers, with all of the libraries and dependencies it needs to run, and then deployed in groups called Pods. A Pod is composed of all of the components required to run an application for an end user. Pods can run single or multiple containers that are needed to deliver a specific set of services through an application. The "one-container-per-Pod" model is very common for Kubernetes use cases.

When pods run multiple containers, they are typically separate services that need to work together in order to deliver a specific experience within an application. This a more advanced use case for container orchestration but becomes more common as applications are broken down into services and micro services.

Google Cloud provides CaaS to clients through its console and abstracts away the complexity of managing operating systems. In the world of CaaS, clients may still want to manage the runtime environment itself but don't need the burden of provisioning specific VMs and their operating systems. This enables additional value and functionality for them, such as autoscaling infrastructure, which can optimize cost relative to traffic while ensuring applications aren't overloaded with traffic relative to their current hardware capacity.

The orchestration of containers, their Pods, and the underlying infrastructure is done by an open source technology called Kubernetes. **Kubernetes** is a service that makes it easy for the technology team to provision and manage VMs at scale with automation. Kubernetes can kill VMs that are dysfunctional while ensuring that duplicate nodes and pods can handle the traffic without impacting the customer experience. It can also scale the clusters based on alerts and traffic signals.

We'll dive deeper into these concepts in *Part 3* of this book, starting with *Chapter 8*.

Functions and FaaS

Functions, similar to containers, are a new way of developing, managing, and serving code. Functions are also small bits of code, similar to microservices, that usually serve a specific and simple purpose. They are very useful in circumstances such as event-based computing, where an event triggers a snippet of code to run and perform a specific task. FaaS solutions abstract away more of the infrastructure and management thereof than PaaS offerings, but you still are responsible for the code itself.

This approach to developing code makes it very easy for developers to quickly write, update, and deploy code. This approach is great when an organization has a small development team or would like to focus resources on development. They can prioritize the launch of code without having to build specific competence around managing Kubernetes and clusters like you would with a CaaS service.

The tradeoff for FaaS offering, similar to the themes we learned about earlier in this chapter, is that you will have little to no control over the underlying infrastructure. The scaling of the infrastructure that runs your function is completely dependent on the FaaS provider.

When designing systems for the cloud, many architectures make sense based on the needs of the client and the cost of the infrastructure. Some components of an application may be hosted via PaaS or FaaS, while some applications may be monolithic and hosted in IaaS environments. At the end of the day, organizations and their engineering teams must weigh the pros and cons of the different hosting models and make the appropriate decision regarding how to approach development and hosting for their applications.

Summary

The different cloud hosting models have evolved to address different needs. SaaS is ideal for business user-facing applications, while developers typically opt for PaaS solutions or even FaaS solutions. Organizations that work in regulated industries and need to have more control and visibility into the underlying infrastructure will build on top of IaaS or CaaS services as they can define specific parameters for the infrastructure, such as the physical locations of where VMs and data will be hosted.

Most organizations weave together solutions that are built on top of the different models to satisfy the needs of the business and build a robust technology ecosystem. Understanding the responsibility of the provider and the responsibility of the client is critical in differentiating between when an IaaS solution would be appropriate versus a PaaS or SaaS system.

To understand why organizations would go through the process of building large technology footprints, we have to understand the value of data to an organization. Data is at the heart of digital transformation and the adoption of cloud systems. In the next chapter, we'll dive deeper into the role of data in transforming organizations while also highlighting the specific Google Cloud systems available today that help with the ingestion, transformation, visualization, and monetization of data.

Part 2:
Innovating with Data and Google Cloud

In the second part of this book, we dive deeper into data specifically, exploring its role in helping companies transform themselves. We'll discuss the data life cycle and relevant Google Cloud products that help customers build mature, reliable data infrastructure. We'll also touch on the innovations in the space, with a particular focus on machine learning and AI.

This part has the following chapters:

- *Chapter 4, The Role of Data in Digital Transformation*
- *Chapter 5, Google Cloud Solutions for Data Management*
- *Chapter 6, Machine Learning and Artificial Intelligence on Google Cloud*

4

The Role of Data in Digital Transformation

Data has become central to the strategic future of many companies across industries. *The Economist* highlighted as far back as 2017 how data had overtaken oil as the most valuable resource in the world, highlighted by the fact that the five most valuable publicly traded firms in the world were all technology companies: **Alphabet**, **Amazon**, **Apple**, **Facebook**, and **Microsoft** (`https://www.economist.com/leaders/2017/05/06/the-worlds-most-valuable-resource-is-no-longer-oil-but-data`). Whether it's using data to surface more relevant search results, ads, content, or products, technology companies were able to harness the power of digitization and data maturity to develop capabilities that helped better understand their customers, shifts in demand, and how to best serve their clients.

In this chapter, we'll explore the following topics:

- The role of data in digital transformation
- The importance of data-driven culture
- The impact of the cloud on data

The role of data in digital transformation

As we learned in the first section of this book, digital transformation allows organizations to rethink how they interact with their clients and service them. Where paper processes dominated, organizations began to adopt digital systems that can more easily consume, manipulate, and showcase information. This transformation allowed business leaders to have a much broader and more accurate understanding of the business as a whole given that data fidelity and availability significantly improved.

The adoption of digital systems played a large role in ensuring that processes that may have been slow, laborious, and expensive were automated, empowering employees to be more productive and less prone to error. Imagine doing math exclusively by hand versus using a calculator. As a human being, you may be able to solve math problems in your head faster than you can type them, assuming the problems aren't too complex and your mind is energized and nourished. However, imagine having to do hundreds of math problems continuously for 8 hours straight. Your vision may begin to blur as you struggle to maintain concentration over such a long period and small mistakes begin to materialize in your work. Perhaps you didn't get enough sleep and where to place the decimal point seems less urgent than taking the next coffee break or imagining your favorite place to take a nap.

Between the capacity for human error, constraints on the time and effort required to complete certain tasks, and the complexity of orchestrating human work with large, complex calculations, computers became the ultimate productivity machine. Applications were developed that could visualize, manipulate, and publish data so that people could more easily interact with information. At their most basic level, all applications are data manipulation engines. They allow you to take data from somewhere, do something to it, and put it somewhere else. This pattern is repeated with additional complexity across applications but fundamentally, the purpose of all applications is to manipulate data.

If your company is a gaming company, gaming applications take input data from users (keystrokes, mouse clicks, pressing a button on a gaming controller) and trigger specific events in the virtual world they've created. This means that whenever a player presses X to speak to a character in a game, they are essentially accessing data that contains the conversation flow for that character based on the fact that they've met a certain set of conditions in a game.

If your company is in the financial services industry, your banking application organizes and visualizes data related to financial transactions for your customers. You visualize both credits and debits for them in their checking accounts, usually in real time, giving your customers full visibility into their current financial posture. The banking application visualizes information related to checking accounts, savings accounts, credit cards, and potentially even vehicle and mortgage loans.

If your company is in the e-commerce industry, your e-commerce application surfaces product information for your clients and creates a virtual storefront from which they can see what inventory you have in stock, the cost of the inventory, and even how long it would take to make a shipment. All of these systems, such as product inventory, logistics, and pricing information, are fundamentally surfacing data that can be cross-referenced to provide a more accurate representation of reality.

Therefore, data is at the heart of digital transformation as the goal of digital transformation is to increase productivity, reduce costs, and create new streams of revenue.

Let's consider an example of a farmer looking to sell their grain and explore how, through digital transformation, their experience can be significantly improved.

The farmer's journey – digitally transformed

After harvesting their wheat, a farmer needs to drop it off at a grain elevator to monetize their inventory. The price of wheat varies by the second as commodity prices fluctuate based on domestic and international factors. Unfortunately, the market price of wheat is low relative to historic prices but the farmer doesn't have much of a choice; the almanac they read predicted that prices would be stable this year, so they decided to sell it at the going market rate.

The farmer drives their truck to the grain elevator and has to wait a few hours before their turn. Once they arrive at the scale, where the truck's weight is measured before and after the grain is dropped off, they receive a paper slip confirming the amount of grain dropped off, along with the price. The farmer then proceeds to wait 3 weeks to receive a check in the mail.

Assuming the check was for the correct amount, all is well in the world. What happens if we introduce some risk or human error into the situation? What if the check that was mailed to the farmer is lost or stolen in transit? What if the amount of the check is incorrect? What if the farmer needs to prove that the amount is incorrect but they can't find the scale receipt from when the grain was dropped off? What if the farmer needed the money within a few days to pay for a loan or mortgage?

The traditional, paper-based processes have multiple points of failure, many of which can end up having a significant negative impact on people's lives. Let's explore a scenario where the farmer is working with digital tools.

While finishing off their harvest, a farmer opens up an application on their phone to look at wheat prices and prepare to drop off the grain. They receive a notification that wheat prices are likely to jump 10% to 20% next week as an international incident impacts prices. They schedule an appointment to drop off the grain at the elevator at a specific time next week and sell their wheat at a premium to speculators betting on the increase at a 5% premium. The transaction is automated so that it can be processed as soon as the buyer signs off on the sale and the grain is dropped off, with the funds hitting the farmer's account shortly after.

Within a digital reimagining of grain transactions, the farmer not only saves time dropping off the grain by scheduling an appointment ahead of time but also is better informed on world events and can make financial decisions based on these events in real time to ensure they get the most value out of their work. They can fully benefit from digital financial services, having real-time visibility and projections for commodity prices, which empowers them to make a more informed decision on when to sell and whom to sell to.

Now that we have a better understanding of data and how it's related to digital transformations, let's dig into the organizational changes driven by digital systems through the rise of data-driven culture.

The importance of data-driven culture

Implementing digital systems and processes is a critical step in maturing an organization's data strategy, but this transformation also necessitates a change in human behavior. The rise of data-driven cultures within organizations is also required for a full digital transformation. This means that people within the organization are willing to invest the time and energy required to implement the appropriate systems, manage them with operational excellence, and deliver value across the company.

An organization that has a strong, data-driven culture will have senior leaders who are committed to making decisions using data and creating a culture where data is valued and used across the organization. Their teams will have data literacy – a basic understanding of what data is made available across the organization and how it should be used. This includes adopting best practices for how to collect, clean, and interpret data and implementing governance controls to ensure that data is accurate, reliable, and accessible where it's appropriate.

Data-driven culture affords organizations several advantages; they can make better decisions, improve efficiency and productivity, identify new opportunities, reduce risk, and gain competitive advantages.

Making better decisions

Making decisions can be very challenging, particularly in larger organizations. There are a large variety of factors that can impact the decision-making process and the consequences may impact people all over the world. By implementing a data-driven approach to making decisions, leadership teams can ensure that their decisions are grounded in reality and reflect the current state of the business and their industry.

For example, if you need to decide whether your business should focus on expansion into Europe, Africa, or Asia, what considerations would you make? You may think of the expansion based on the total addressable market, the nature of the competitive landscape, the cost of establishing operations, and the risk related to legal or national security issues. Much of this analysis may be done based on external information that is available via the internet from sources such as news outlets, academic journals, or research published by consultants.

Assuming you did not have a data-driven culture inside your organization, what might influence that decision? Perhaps which part of the world executives prefer to travel to or where they have existing relationships. Perhaps it would be which market is perceived to be the most deregulated or where governments may be the most malleable.

Within a data-driven organization, however, leadership should prioritize what data is available to the organization and use that to make decisions. Where has their organization seen the most traction, what market has the highest growth rate, and what is the customer acquisition cost in these different markets relative to how much revenue they can drive? Rather than make decisions based on bias, emotion, or other human factors, executives should be making decisions based on information – which ideally should be recent, validated, and relevant.

Improving productivity and efficiency

Productivity and efficiency are major benefactors of digital transformation and data-driven cultures. Organizations that adopt digital systems and automate processes often see significant improvement in output per employee. By implementing systems and processes that reduce toil and repetitive tasks, people can focus their time and energy on tasks more suited for human beings, such as creativity, critical thinking, and innovation.

As organizations transitioned from typewriters to personal computers, the amount of time it took to write letters was significantly reduced. We transitioned from physical mail to email, where messages were sent and received at the speed of light with the click of a button. Tasks that could've taken weeks to orchestrate and execute can now be completed in a matter of hours or minutes. For example, working on a presentation may require collaboration across several different business units. In a non-digital world, this collaboration would require the coordination of multiple teams as they refine their content and work to deliver a cohesive narrative to the leadership team. This may mean hours of meetings as folks build out the presentation and get feedback from their respective teams and leadership before ultimately finalizing the content.

In the world of today, using cloud-native tools such as Google Workspace, you can create a slide deck, assign sections of it to different teams, and dynamically collaborate over the internet. If teams don't overlap time zones, they can even add comments to other sections of the presentation and ensure that their feedback is taken into consideration. Not only is information more easily accessible, but this creates an environment where collaboration becomes effortless and tools are leveraged to lubricate the interaction of different teams.

Identifying new opportunities

Data-driven culture also has the benefit of helping organizations and their leadership teams identify new opportunities to better serve their customers. Once information is digital and easily available, teams across the organization can cross-reference different bodies of information to find patterns and outliers in the data. For example, an e-commerce firm may cross-reference weather data with marketing campaigns to launch a campaign for rain boots and umbrellas whenever it rains. A data platform company may provide analytics or advanced capabilities such as machine learning as a service to its clients.

Digitization opens up all kinds of new ways to monetize as organizations begin to rethink how they go to market, how they price and package their products, and who their customers are. As a gaming company, perhaps that's identifying a new market where you are seeing outsized growth and doubling down on that market. As an advertiser, that may be identifying a campaign that is performing well within a specific audience and identifying other people who have similar interests to that audience and running the campaign against them as well. For a healthcare organization, it may mean carrying out patient population studies to identify who is at the highest risk for specific health conditions, such as type 2 diabetes within those populations, and launching preventative health programs.

Data gives us a new lens through which to look at a business and businesses that have a strong data culture, mature data systems, and practices will have an advantage over those that do not.

Gaining a competitive advantage

Data generated by an organization is a valuable resource that can be weaponized to gain a competitive advantage. Variables such as deal sizes, revenue by market, and growth are all inputs that can be taken into account when designing go-to-market strategies to better compete with the rest of the market.

Similarly, data that is collected from customers can be used to inform product development and strategy. By running rigorous client evaluations, organizations can collect client sentiment in real time and leverage that information to gain an advantage over competitors. This information can range from sentiment related to brand, technology, and what it's like to work with employees from your company.

Organizations that can collect, analyze, and implement client feedback faster than others will have advantages in both client satisfaction and capability. A data-centric culture ensures that teams within your organization will not only respect client feedback but also respect the process of acting on client feedback. This will usually entail the implementation of client satisfaction measuring systems such as the Net Promoter Score, where the likelihood of a client referring the solution to someone else is measured rather than just raw satisfaction. In addition, there will need to be client feedback looks implemented, such as feature requests and development engagements.

In summary, developing and implementing a data-driven culture for an organization gives it many advantages over its competitors that do not follow suit. They'll be able to make better-informed decisions by using reliable and up-to-date data that empowers them to be more productive and efficient and identify new opportunities. By identifying and making the most of these opportunities, they'll be able to out-innovate their competition, building features and capabilities that provide meaningful value to clients and therefore generate expansion and net new opportunities.

The impact of the cloud on data

The cloud revolution has significant implications for how data is stored, accessed, and used. Historically, the usability of data had real-world limits, such as how many pieces of paper could fit in a filing cabinet, how many cabinets you could fit in a closet, and how well-documented the filing system was. Moving on from paper filing systems, organizations ran into data accessibility issues when supporting distributed workforces.

Although a file may be digitized, depending on how it is stored, it may not be accessible. For example, a salesperson may want access to the historical performance of their territory to build a territory plan for the coming fiscal year. Ideally, they would want visibility into the last 5 years of their transaction history, including the names of clients and the deal sizes. This information would help inform them of where and with whom their product has had traction, which, in turn, would help them define a strategy for the year.

What if this data wasn't easily available in the cloud through a customer management system? This may have meant having to coordinate with business analysts, IT, and data engineers to define the scope of the data request and gain formal approval. What should be a simple process of manipulating a report in the cloud becomes a multi-team effort for a simple data request.

Let's explore the impact that the cloud has had on data across a few areas.

Increased scalability and flexibility

By leveraging cloud systems, organizations can better manage and dynamically scale their data. Assuming they need to grow their capacity for a specific project, they can build out storage projects in the public cloud and get instant access to petabytes, if not exabytes, of storage. This usage can also be scaled down based on need, assuming some of the projects they are working on are time-bound and involve the purging of data once a task is completed.

Cloud systems also allow an infrastructure team to make the best decision relative to a workload for how to architect a system. Perhaps they need a multi-cloud or hybrid architecture and many modern data systems are being built with this flexibility in mind as they abstract away the underlying infrastructure and allow you to use the solution across multiple backend environments.

Improved data security

Data systems that are built on top of public cloud providers also benefit from the maturity and security of the underlying infrastructure. As we explored in *Chapter 3* with the **shared responsibility model**, organizations can offload physical infrastructure security to cloud providers. Their internal teams can focus on building and securing the code and application itself, allowing them to specialize in launching secure and performant code.

Many organizations struggle to implement and maintain a robust security practice from a technology perspective. By leveraging cloud systems, they can ensure that their data has a baseline of meaningful physical security and lighten the load on their technology teams. In Google Cloud, for example, all data is encrypted at rest and in transit by default. Normally, this would have to be manually implemented and configured by a technology team.

Reduced costs

The shift to cloud systems for managing and manipulating data also has cost implications. When leveraging a public cloud provider such as Google Cloud, clients benefit from the fact that Google can procure IT equipment at a massive scale. This usually translates into better rates for equipment and software from manufacturers who sell these products in bulk. Google is then able to pass on the cost savings from procuring the hardware and software in bulk to its clients through the platform.

For example, if you were to procure one server from a server manufacturer, it may cost $10,000. Meanwhile, if you were to procure 1,000 servers from that manufacturer, they may charge you $5,000 per server. Effectively, the hardware is procured at 50% of the list cost in bulk, at which point you can make that hardware available to your clients as a service.

In addition, given the flexibility of cloud systems, clients are empowered to pay for infrastructure that they use based on how much data they store and how much data is processed. By contrast, assuming you are building out your own data center, you would be at the mercy of the hardware and software costs once it is procured. If you buy a petabyte of storage, you have a petabyte of storage, whether or not the capacity is used.

Improved collaboration

Cloud systems add an additional layer of value to digitized information. Once data is in the cloud, it becomes accessible to anyone with the appropriate permission and access to the internet. Workers are no longer tied to physical machines and have to save their work to the local drive of their work computer. Files are stored in cloud-based data repositories and can be accessed from any device. This has implications for teams who may need to work together across geographies and time zones.

Similar to our presentation example from earlier, imagine having to build a presentation for the leadership team that requires collaboration between finance, legal, marketing, and sales. With cloud-based systems such as Google Slides and a **customer relationship management** (**CRM**) system, sales can create a slide deck, build out the different sections, comment specific people into specific slides, and ask them to populate or validate data. They can even pull reports from the CRM system on the historical performance of their territory and use it to inform their strategy.

As work culture continues to evolve from *working at the office* to *working from anywhere*, employees want to be empowered to work from multiple devices and locations. Through cloud productivity systems, they can work from their laptop or their phone, from the comfort of their home, office, or even a ship sailing across the Atlantic.

Increased innovation

The adoption of cloud systems not only increases the ability to innovate but also the pace of innovation. Much of the value of landing data in the cloud is making it accessible across the company to empower employees to drive new ways of working and by extension delivering services to customers.

Folks who adopt cloud-native systems and pursue data-centric innovation will be marrying datasets from across their business to surface new insights. Perhaps this means a shift from demographic targeting to behavioral targeting, where you target your marketing campaigns not on zip codes or age but on online behavior. At a gaming company, this may mean cross-referencing purchasing behavior with user surveys to understand what promotions your customers want to see and how they like to interact with those promotions.

Summary

In conclusion, the advent of cloud computing is unlocking new ways to store, transform, analyze, and derive value from data. Not only is data easier to handle in the cloud, empowering teams to define, implement, and enforce security policies, but it also enables collaboration and innovation. Organizations that make the most of their data and leverage the innovation being driven by Google in its cloud platform through technologies such as the Vertex AI platform will create new streams of revenue or new ways to solve old problems. Both adopting a strong data culture and cloud-native data architecture, companies will not only be able to think like Google but also build like Google – for planetary scale and accessibility with a strong security posture and compliance controls.

Now that we have a better understanding of how data, the cloud, and a data-driven culture impact an organization, in the next chapter, we'll be digging into Google Cloud's solutions for data management across both structured and unstructured data.

5

Google Cloud Solutions for Data Management

Handling data in production is no small feat, and organizations weave together a symphony of services in order to build ingestion pipelines, transformation pipelines, **machine learning** (**ML**) training pipelines, data lakes, and data warehouses. Establishing a mature data culture in an organization entails the adoption of practices that may be new for technology teams and often involves the adoption of new technologies. These technologies often range from first-party cloud vendor-provided technologies to third-party licensed software, all the way to **open source software** (**OSS**). Larger organizations and even more mature start-ups will need to understand data architecture, the landscape of solutions, and cost-to-performance trade-offs relative to the application that will be serviced.

In this chapter, we will provide an overview of the data management solutions available on Google Cloud from both a functional and a capability perspective. We will follow along the data life cycle as we cover everything from ingestion to processing and serving data.

Here is a summary of what will be covered:

- Understanding the data journey
- Exploring types of data
- Elaborating on Google Cloud solutions for data management

Understanding the data journey

The first step of manipulating data in the cloud is to upload the data to a cloud environment. Depending on the source system and the volume of data, different approaches can be taken. For small file uploads, for example, it may be as simple as using the user interface of Google Cloud to upload a file to a storage bucket. However, as data volumes grow, this simple GUI-based upload may not make sense. Google Cloud customers can also upload data to the cloud via a couple of methods: a transfer over the internet or via a transfer appliance.

The most convenient way of transferring data is generally doing so over the internet, and typically, this is the preferred method. Assuming there are reasons why you can't do the transfer online, either because of bandwidth limitations or cost, customers can opt to do a transfer via hardware. For the transfer appliance, customers receive a physical storage server that is meant to be hydrated with corporate data that will be uploaded to the cloud.

These methods sound great if you're working with static data, but what if you need to update it relatively frequently, such as daily or monthly, or even need real-time data? That's where data pipelines come into play. An **ingestion pipeline** is a process where a system calls data from a source system and lands it in a destination system. This can be done autonomously and at scale via APIs as part of an automated ingestion pipeline.

The primary way to ingest data into Google Cloud when building automated data pipelines is with Pub/Sub. **Pub/Sub** is a serverless autoscaling data ingestion service that is great for ingesting data from multiple sources and is able to land the data across multiple services. For example, Pub/Sub may call APIs from a **customer relationship management system** (**CRM**) and a marketing system and land that data in a Cloud Storage bucket for archival or retention purposes. It may also push the data to a transformation pipeline where it will be sanitized before arriving at its final destination: a data warehouse where it can be consumed by other systems or employees for a specific business purpose. Some advantages of Pub/Sub include its **high availability** (**HA**) across regions, at-least-once message delivery with support for both push and pull modes, and its ability to handle real-time data.

Sometimes, customers may depend on a third-party or open source version of the ingesting solution, and the most common one is **Apache Kafka**. Kafka is an open source distributed streaming platform that is used to ingest large volumes of data from multiple systems. It can also be used or procured through **independent software vendors** (**ISVs**) who offer managed versions of Kafka such as Confluent and Aiven, which offer a hardened version of the software with some level of infrastructure abstraction where clusters can scale based on need or load.

Once data is in the cloud, ingestion services will typically land the data in a transformation pipeline where the data is cleaned and structured in a way that will be in harmony with the rest of the data in a datastore. Alternatively or simultaneously, the ingested data may need to be stored in a data lake where it may be retained in its raw format for retention or even compliance-related purposes.

A **data lake** in the world of cloud computing is a central repository of data that is used to store large volumes of data in its native format. Data lakes are typically built on top of object storage services. **Google Cloud Storage** (**GCS**) is an example of an object storage service, and the benefit of this type of storage is that it can handle any file type, be it structured, semi-structured, or unstructured data. Beyond being flexible in that it can store all file types, cloud-based object storage buckets are also scalable and cost-effective when compared to other datastores. The size of storage buckets can be dynamic and grow or shrink relative to how much data is in the bucket. Companies don't have to provision a certain number of servers or compute capacity to address the growth of the data; it's purely a storage service with no compute component, allowing for very cost-effective data storage.

Let's assume that Pub/Sub sent data to both a data lake for long-term retention and a data pipeline for processing. Once the data is forked and sent to a transformation pipeline, this will typically kick off an **extract, transform, and load** (ETL) or **extract, load, and transform** (ELT) process. These acronyms denote whether data is transformed before or after landing at its destination. Within Google Cloud, the most common services used for ETL jobs are **Dataflow** and **Dataproc**. We'll go deeper into those two services later on in the chapter, but for now, we should think of Dataflow as a serverless Apache Beam service that handles both real-time and batch transformation jobs. Meanwhile, Dataproc can be thought of as serverless Apache Spark. Apache Beam and Spark are both open source projects for data processing.

Once data is cleaned through an automated data pipeline via Dataflow or Dataproc, for example, it is then landed in one or multiple systems for consumption. If this data is externally facing or is business-critical data for business operations, it may land in a database. If the data is intended to be used by data science, business analyst teams, or visualization, it may land in a data warehouse.

A database is typically defined as a collection of data within a system that is organized and structured in a way that makes it easily searchable and accessible to other systems. In the world of the cloud, the traditional relational database has grown into several different types of datastores based on the type of data and the needs of an application. **Relational databases** are what people typically think of when they think of databases. They store data in tables composed of columns and rows, where each row represents a single record and each column represents a piece of data about that record. A great example of relational data is data that is used as part of a personal banking application. Your account and balance information is highly sensitive and must always be accurate. Adding or removing a 0 from your account balance can have a drastic impact on your financial health. Therefore, this data must be treated with the utmost care to ensure it is consistently accurate and able to change, with an audit trail, based on charges you incur in real time.

Relational databases continue to be used in cloud computing where they make sense. One of the constraints on these kinds of databases is that they must maintain data integrity or be ACID compliant, which means that they can normally only scale vertically—by adding more compute and storage to an existing database. **ACID** is an acronym that stands for **atomicity, consistency, isolation, and durability**. It represents properties that ensure database transactions are processed reliably. When deploying a database that is ACID compliant, you can guarantee that the data in the database will be accurate and reliable, particularly when best practices are adopted, such as backups in order to minimize the impact of unexpected issues.

Maintaining large relational databases can be very expensive given the continuous need to scale the hardware that it's running on, and they struggle to handle global use cases. An example of using a relational database that makes sense is as the backend for a banking application for a small, regional bank. Bank account information must be consistent, durable, and isolated. If, for example, you wake up one day and it turns out the bank accidentally withdrew $10,000 instead of $1,000, it may cause you to miss payments on a mortgage or a car loan, which is unacceptable. By keeping banking data in a relational database, the regional bank can ensure data integrity despite potential errors or failures such as system outages.

Google Cloud has developed a relational database that can overcome some of the challenges associated with relational databases. **Spanner** is able to scale horizontally or across multiple nodes, while still retaining its ACID compliance. We'll go deeper into what this means later in the chapter, but for now, it's important to be aware that not all relational databases are created equal. Customers who opt for a traditional relational database on Google Cloud will typically use the Cloud SQL service, which supports MySQL and PostgreSQL, both open source projects, or Microsoft SQL Server.

When use cases arise where a relational database won't be appropriate for the application, either because the data is not structured properly or the cost-to-performance ratios don't make sense, for example, customers can use non-relational databases.

Non-relational databases or **NoSQL databases** have a different way of storing and organizing data for retrieval. Rather than storing data in tables with columns and rows, data may be stored as key-value pairs, documents, or graphs. A **key-value datastore** is used to describe a system that uses a key as a unique identifier with which a plethora of other data can be stored across a variety of formats. An example of when this makes sense is gaming session data. The username becomes the key, and values that are paired with the key may be current health, world map location, item skins, and statistics associated with the current game state. They are generally great for caching, session management, and storing simple data. A great example of a key-value pair datastore is Memorystore, which is Google Cloud's managed offering of Redis. Redis is often used to store game and session data in gaming applications. The key would be the user ID, and the values associated with the key could be location on a map, what items are in the inventory, and how much health a character has at a specific point in time in the game.

Document databases are great for storing semi-structured data such as documents. They tend to be more flexible than key-value datastores, but they're also not as fast at retrieving and storing data. They can also be searched based on the content of the documents rather than by just the key. They make great backends for document repositories or storing semi-structured data such as JSON documents. **Firestore** is a great example of a document-oriented database that is able to handle real-time data and is easy to get up and running. It's fully serverless, allowing it to scale up and down to meet demand, which makes it a great backend for semi-structured search use cases such as searching inside documents.

Graph databases store data in a network of nodes and edges known as a graph. Each node represents an entity, while each edge represents a relation between two entities. When there are multiple entities with complex relationships to each other, graph databases are optimal for addressing the use case. They are very common when addressing the needs of social networking applications, fraud detection systems, and recommendation engines. This is powerful when recommending content to users as graph databases are able to inform the engine on the nuances of a person's interests. Knowing that a user was born in Boston and has friends who like football, it may recommend content on the *New England Patriots* for that user.

Both relational and non-relational databases are great ways to store data and make sense to implement based on the specific needs of the business, application, or customer. We typically think of data in a database as *hot* data or data that needs to be readily accessible at any moment. That data may need to be accessible by a customer, such as checking bank account information, or an employee who is searching for a legal document that outlines a specific policy.

Assuming data needs to be made available to a data science team, however, databases may not be the most efficient or cost-effective way to store data. When we get into the world of big data, where data scientists may need access to a petabyte of data if not more, databases may not be able to handle the scale. Between being able to serve vast amounts of data and the cost pressure from running traditional datastores, the concept of a data warehouse was born.

A **data warehouse** is a central repository of ideally clean data that can be used for analysis, reporting, and ML use cases. It is typically architected in a way that makes it highly scalable while still being able to quickly and efficiently perform queries. Google Cloud's **BigQuery**, for example, has decoupled the compute and storage components of the technology, allowing for the storage to scale dynamically while only leveraging compute as needed by queries. BigQuery also allows data teams to partition the data, allowing for queries to run on only parts of the datasets in the system, which also significantly improves query speed while minimizing cost. Warehouses are also able to serve as a landing or staging zone for chaotic data. Customers can land data in the warehouse before transforming it, known as an ELT process. This flexibility makes them great at handling semi-structured data and as a staging step for production data.

Because storing data in data warehouses is very cost-efficient, customers can marry datasets that previously would've been isolated due to a lack of system integration or cross-team collaboration. If you are a software company, you can enrich historical sales data with marketing campaign information, real-time sales data, customer surveys, and third-party datasets. This big data approach to understanding a business can be really powerful as leadership can make decisions based on a deeper, richer, data-driven lens rather than one clouded by stale, disjointed, or erroneous data.

Data warehouses also make great backends for visualization tools such as Google Cloud's **Looker**. Given the variety of data and the cost-effective nature of data warehouses, implementing tools such as Looker enables folks from across the business to self-serve data as needed rather than having to go through analysts for reports and dashboards. Looker dashboards and reports can be leveraged internally or even embedded in external applications for external consumption. Whether you target this toward customers, partners, or internal teams, visualization and reporting tools are a great way to communicate with folks to help them understand the data that is available and extract value from it.

Now that we've followed along the data journey from ingestion through to visualization, let's go back through the main components by way of a case study.

Acme e-commerce – case study

You are the director of e-commerce for a traditional retailer and want to mature your company's data practices and digital posture. The company has been in business for 20 years and specializes in selling novelty hats. These hats are typically available in brick-and-mortar locations in shopping malls around the nation, but only 20% of your business is done online.

You want to launch an online campaign to drive more traffic to your website, but before you do that, you want to have an understanding of the purchasing patterns of your customers so that you know what to market and to whom.

In order to have an understanding of historical customer purchasing patterns, you need to partner with a number of teams across your business. You need data from the **point-of-sale** (**POS**) system to have visibility into real-time purchasing behavior. You also need to connect with inventory teams to have visibility into what inventory is available and being procured based on the different geographic regions that you serve. You also want to consolidate all of this data with consumer surveys that have been conducted over the past 6 months and historical sales information.

Consolidating all of this data seems daunting, but you set out to build a data lake! A data lake will allow you to have all of these different datasets in one place that you can use as a staging area. As a good director of e-commerce, you naturally catalog and organize the datasets in your cloud storage bucket to ensure your data lake stays a lake and doesn't become a swamp.

Next, you task your team to massage all of this data and flatten it out so that it can be landed in a data warehouse. Eventually, you plan to build automated data pipelines to handle data exports periodically from all of these systems, but to start, just exporting historical data is enough.

Once all of the data is cleaned and landed in the data warehouse, you start to run queries and generate reports from the system. In your investigation, you notice that for some reason, the marketing team has been running a campaign in your West Coast market for a product that is out of stock. You inform the inventory and marketing teams, letting them know that they either need to increase inventory or change the campaign; otherwise, the marketing dollars would be wasted.

Good job! You just saved the company $100,000 that would've been wasted on a campaign for a product that's out of stock! This would have not only been a $0 conversion campaign, with customers unable to add the item to the shopping cart, but also such a bad experience for the customers that they may no longer have trusted your site for online shopping and decided to go to your competitors to service their needs.

This oversimplified case study helps highlight how the unification and analysis of data from disparate systems can provide meaningful insights to a business. Whether it's identifying inefficiencies or new opportunities, data helps us understand how a business is performing in the real world and highlights areas of improvement.

Now that we understand the journey that data follows within a cloud-native architecture and how businesses can derive value from it, let's explore some of the variables that impact how data is handled, used, and stored.

Exploring types of data

When working with cloud systems and data, it's important to have a deep understanding of what data is available, how it is stored, which systems can access it, and how the data is being used. By having a holistic understanding of a company's data ecosystem, team members are able to identify where it makes sense to re-architect systems or consolidate datasets based on business needs.

There are a few underlying concepts that need to be covered to ensure you understand what type of data makes up a dataset and what variables to consider when designing the architecture of a system that may try to derive value from the data through analysis or predictions. Let's start by exploring the different types of data—structured, semi-structured, and unstructured—while also defining some of the considerations when making decisions about how to use, store, transform, and serve it.

Structured data is data that is organized in a schema, or predefined structure, which makes it easy to store, query, and analyze. The most common characterization of it is to think of structured data as data that fits easily into a table or a spreadsheet. The data is organized in rows and columns, where the row represents a record and columns designate a specific attribute for each record. This may be a name with a birth date or tracking a sales number across 12 months for a specific representative. Structured data is very common in applications and is typically used and stored in relational databases and data warehouses. An example of a file format for structured data is **CSV**, which stands for **comma-separated values**, and the data within those files may contain customer records, financial transactions, or scientific data.

Semi-structured data is described as datasets that have some level of structure but are not necessarily as easily stored and organized in tables as structured data. Common file formats for semi-structured data include XML or JSON. Examples of semi-structured data include email messages, web pages, social media posts, or sensor data. This kind of data may need to be transformed or flattened out in order to land in a data warehouse, for example, to do analysis across datasets.

Unstructured data is data that has no predefined format, and it can be the most difficult to store, query, and analyze given the wide variety of file types, formats, and content. This data is composed of files such as text documents, images, and audio and video files. They may be very large, with videos and photos being great examples, and therefore don't make sense to store in a database. Alternatively, they may just be documents generated by employees containing important internal information such as legal and corporate policies, which include long-form text and image files such as workflow diagrams or charts. If clients need to fill out any forms, either by hand or online, this information may be critical to land in a database, but the form itself may be an unstructured data file and therefore require processing to extract variables from it before landing that data specifically into a database.

As companies build a catalog of data, understanding what data they have, where it resides, and in what format, they'll start to understand how to process it in order to derive value for the business or clients.

In the next section of this chapter, we'll dig deeper into what options exist for data storage, processing, and life-cycle management on Google Cloud while highlighting specific use cases and competitors for each service.

Elaborating on Google Cloud solutions for data management

In this section of the chapter, we will review each of the first-party and Google-managed open source offerings available on Google Cloud. We will provide a brief description of each service while highlighting the use case and comparative solutions or potential competitors. We'll start with the data pipeline services, covering ingestion and transformation, before covering data lakes, datastores, and beyond.

The following diagram highlights a high-level overview of Google Cloud-native data analytics pipeline leveraging exclusively first-party or Google-managed open source technologies:

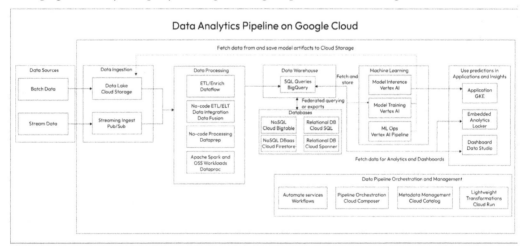

Figure 5.1 – Mature data pipeline in Google Cloud (source: https://storage.googleapis.com/gweb-cloudblog-publish/images/Data_Analytics_Pipeline_on_Google_CLoud.max-1500x1500.png)

We'll start on the left side, covering ingestion through to transformation, before finishing with data warehousing and visualization in this chapter. We'll dive into the ML components of this architecture in the next chapter.

Data pipelines

Data pipelines are automated tasks woven together to ingest, transform, and land data in the appropriate datastores. Within the world of Google Cloud, this is typically broken down into two types of data pipeline functions: ingestion and transformation. For ingestion, the main tool that's available from Google Cloud is **Pub/Sub**. For transformation, Google Cloud makes available two open source projects that are provided as a managed service. **Dataflow** provides clients with a managed offering of **Apache Beam**, while **Dataproc** provides clients with a managed offering of **Apache Spark**. In the subsections ahead, we'll highlight the core function of the services along with a description and comparable solutions.

Pub/Sub

Let us review Pub/Sub:

- **Description**: Fully managed, autoscaling, real-time multi-in and multi-out messaging service. It's able to handle the ingestion of large volumes of data across multiple systems and is able to push that data to multiple systems, all while scaling dynamically to handle the load.

- **Use case**: Data ingestion; supports batch and streaming.

- **Competitors**: Apache Kafka, Amazon Kinesis Data Firehose.

Dataflow

Let us review Dataflow:

- **Description**: Fully managed autoscaling service for executing data transformations and building data pipelines. It is essentially a deployment of Apache Beam on Google Cloud, able to handle both batch and stream data processing. It's also easy to integrate with the rest of Google Cloud, such as Pub/Sub and Cloud Storage.

- **Use case**: Data transformation, stream and batch data processing (Beam).

- **Competitors**: Azure HDInsight, Amazon Kinesis Data Analytics.

Dataproc

Let us review Dataproc:

- **Description**: Fully managed autoscaling service for executing data transformation and building data pipelines. Dataproc can be thought of as an Apache Spark service managed by Google and handles both batch and stream processing jobs.

- **Use case**: Batch and stream data processing (Spark).

- **Competitors**: Azure HDInsight, Amazon EMR.

Cloud Composer

Let us review Cloud Composer:

- **Description**: Fully managed pipeline orchestration service that allows you to author, schedule, and monitor data pipelines across all environments, including other clouds and hybrid environments. It's essentially a Google-managed deployment of Apache Airflow on Google Cloud.

- **Use case**: Data pipeline orchestration.

- **Competitors**: Azure Data Factory, AWS Data Pipeline.

Workflows

Let us review Workflows:

- **Description**: Fully managed and serverless workflow orchestration service that can weave together both Google Cloud services and third-party APIs for event-driven execution.

- **Use case**: Automate processes that are event-driven and may constitute both GCP services and third-party APIs.

- **Competitors**: Apache Airflow, Argo Workflows.

Data Fusion

Let us review Data Fusion:

- **Description**: GUI-based fully managed data integration and pipeline development service with 150+ preconfigured connectors and transformations built on top of **Cask Data Application Platform** (**CDAP**) for portability. It allows folks who are less technical to string together services and data pipelines without having to code.

- **Use case**: Design and implement data pipelines through a drag-and-drop interface.

- **Competitors**: AWS Glue, Azure Data Factory.

Data lakes

The term **data lake** refers to a data repository where a large amount of data is stored and organized in a way that makes it easy to understand which files exist, what sources they came from, and relevant attributes such as dates covered by the datasets and file types. By cataloging data, technology teams can ensure that when folks need access to a specific dataset, it is easy to find and retrieve. The most common datastore for data lakes is object storage, where there are no limitations on what kinds of files can be stored. **Cloud Storage** is the service on Google Cloud that is used for object storage, and it has the ability to retain files in different bucket types depending on how often the data needs to be accessed. This allows for cost optimization relative to data storage and retrieval costs.

Cloud Storage buckets can also be both regional or multi-regional, allowing teams to architect systems in a way that can comply with data residency and compliance restrictions. Google Cloud also makes available a set of services to help transform Cloud Storage buckets into data lakes. This includes **Dataplex** and **Data Catalog**, tools that help with identifying data.

Cloud Storage

Let us review Cloud Storage:

- **Description**: Cloud-based, serverless object storage service with multiple storage classes based on retention and access needs. It's a great repository for all file types and is typically used as the foundational service for building a data lake in Google Cloud. Cloud Storage is also able to dynamically move files to the different classes based on how long a file is in a bucket and whether or not it has been accessed or used. All data, regardless of storage class, is accessible at the speed of light.

  Cloud storage buckets can be either regional or multi-regional, and the storage classes are set out here:

  - **Standard**: Hot data that is frequently accessed or stored for short periods of time.

  - **Nearline**: Lower cost for infrequently accessed data, usually less than once a month.

  - **Coldline**: Very low cost for data that is accessed less than once a quarter.

  - **Archival**: Lowest cost; data is accessed less than once a year.

- **Use case**: General storage, data lake, archives, backup and recovery.

- **Competitors**: **Amazon Simple Storage Service** (**Amazon S3**), Azure Blob Storage, **Azure Data Lake Storage** (**ADLS**).

Dataplex

Let us review Dataplex:

- **Description**: Data fabric solution that unifies data and allows customers to automate data management and governance. Dataplex allows you to build a data mesh across data that may be stored across multiple Google Cloud projects without the need to move data across projects. It helps you discover what data you have and empowers you to manage, monitor, and govern it, allowing you to standardize and unify metadata, security, and governance policies, providing full life-cycle management for distributed data.

- **Use case**: Data governance, discovery, metadata mapping and management.

- **Competitors**: Collibra, OneTrust, Talend.

Databases

Databases are systems that are used to organize and quickly sort through information. By organizing data in a way that's easily retrievable, applications can be built to surface and manipulate data in real time. There are different types of databases, namely relational and non-relational, but there are also more specific variations such as document and caching datastores. **Cloud SQL** and **Spanner** are the two core relational database services, while **Firestore** and **Bigtable** are the core non-relational offerings.

Cloud SQL

Let us review Cloud SQL:

- **Description**: Fully managed relational database service for Google Cloud that supports the deployment of MySQL, PostgreSQL, and Microsoft SQL Server. Data is encrypted at rest and in transit by default, allowing customers to build on a secure foundation. Cloud SQL is also able to replicate data across zones and regions, making it able to handle cross-zonal or regional workloads relatively well, although it will still struggle with globally distributed use cases.
- **Use case**: Regional relational database.
- **Competitors: Amazon Relational Database Service (Amazon RDS)**, Azure SQL Database.

Spanner

Let us review Spanner:

- **Description**: Fully managed distributed relational database service that is able to retain ACID compliance and automatic, synchronous replication despite being horizontally scalable. It is optimal for data that is global in scale and needs to retain strong consistency. Spanner decouples compute and storage resources, allowing for the service to scale the compute and storage dynamically based on needs without throttling read and write capacity. It's also SQL compliant, allowing customers to use a familiar query language.
- **Use case**: Global relational database, airline/flight information, banking applications.
- **Competitors**: CockroachDB.

Firestore

Let us review Firestore:

- **Description**: Fully managed autoscaling NoSQL document database that is ideal for mobile and web applications. Firestore is able to handle real-time data synchronization across multiple devices, making it great for applications that need to keep users updated with data in real time, such as chat applications and gaming.

- **Use case**: Non-relational datastore, document database, gaming session information, social media, and chat apps.
- **Competitors**: Amazon DocumentDB, Azure Cosmos DB.

Bigtable

Let us review Bigtable:

- **Description**: Managed wide-column NoSQL database service that is able to handle both structured and semi-structured data at a petabyte scale. Bigtable is able to deliver sub-millisecond latency and 99.999% availability, making it ideal for large-scale analytical workloads such as clickstream analysis and other time-series use cases such as the **Internet of Things** (**IoT**).
- **Use case**: Non-relational key-value database; highly scalable and performant, ideal for real-time analytics such as ad personalization and IoT data.
- **Competitors**: Apache HBase, Amazon Dynamo DB, Azure CosmosDB, Cassandra.

Memorystore

Let us review Memorystore:

- **Description**: Fully managed in-memory storage service for running Redis and Memcached workloads. The solution is low latency while also being highly scalable and available. This service is great for building applications that require caches and are able to retrieve data with sub-millisecond latency.
- **Use case**: Caching data that needs to be frequently accessed, such as user profiles, product catalogs, and search results.
- **Competitors**: Amazon ElastiCache, Amazon MemoryDB.

Data warehouses

Data warehouses are services that allow for the storage of large amounts of data in a cost-effective manner while also enabling the relatively fast retrieval of data when needed. They typically store significantly more information than a relational database, for example, while still being able to retrieve information economically. They are typically used as organized data repositories that serve as a backend to a visualization system and are also great staging areas or launching points for data science projects and ML.

BigQuery

Let us review BigQuery:

- **Description**: Fully managed first-party data warehouse service for Google Cloud that is highly scalable, easy to use, and cost-effective. BigQuery has a decoupled architecture where it can scale storage and compute dynamically based on need. This also enables BigQuery to be highly performant and cost-effective since customers can scale the compute to handle large queries if needed but only pay for the compute that they use. BigQuery also has built-in ML capabilities, allowing customers to not only use SQL to run queries but also run model predictions on their data. It's also highly available and secure, allowing customers to address compliance restrictions such as enterprise-grade and row-level security.

- **Use case**: Data warehouse, storing large amounts of data for historical analysis and ML model training and predictions.

- **Competitors**: Snowflake, Amazon Redshift.

Business intelligence tools

Business intelligence (BI) tools such as **Looker** empower folks to self-serve, manipulate, and explore data in order to extract business value. Users may be analysts building and scheduling reports for leadership teams or salespersons looking to understand data related to a specific customer they manage. They have both internal and external use cases, whereby a company may use them for internal reporting purposes but also leverage them as an embedded solution for their application, allowing their customers to access and manipulate data through it.

Looker

Let us review Looker:

- **Description**: BI platform that allows customers to derive value from data by integrating with a data warehouse and empowers teams and customers to self-serve data from the platform. It provides a visualization layer for data that folks can use to build and schedule reports and dashboards, increasing the accessibility of data while also ensuring that all appropriate compliance and security controls are in place. Looker has a few different versions: a free tier, an internally facing dashboarding tier, and externally facing dashboards tier.

- **Use case**: Data visualization for internal and external use with controls for security and compliance.

- **Competitors**: Tableau, Sisense, Amazon QuickSight, Power BI.

The data journey requires a symphony of services to be woven together based on how data is formatted, accessed, and used. Depending on the application or use case, a customer may use a relational database for relational data, non-relational databases for non-relational data, and a data warehouse for data science and ML use cases. Understanding when to use one versus the other is a core competency for the *Google Cloud Digital Leader* certification. It's important to know which service applies and when, particularly as it relates to specific use cases.

Summary

Understanding the different services available through the Google Cloud platform, their core functions, and why they would be used is important in order to prepare for the *Google Cloud Digital Leader* certification exam. When going through the questions, often you will be asked what service is the most appropriate based on a set of circumstances and business needs.

Being able to define and differentiate when one service would be used rather than another will be critical in attaining the certification, particularly as we go into the next chapter, which will be focused on the Google Cloud services that are used for ML and **artificial intelligence (AI)**.

You can almost think of ML or AI as automated data science, where algorithms are trained to make decisions or predictions based on historical data. If the data the model is trained on is not properly managed, sanitized, and organized, the quality of the model will suffer.

6

Machine Learning and Artificial Intelligence on Google Cloud

The topics of **machine learning** (**ML**) and **artificial intelligence** (**AI**) are supercharged with societal imagination given the generative arms race that has kicked off between major companies such as Google, Amazon, and Microsoft, along with an ecosystem of model and solution providers such as Anthropic, Cohere, and Copy.ai. In this chapter, you will learn about the history of the usage of ML and AI at Google before we explore what solutions are available through Google Cloud.

By the end of this chapter, you will be able to do the following:

- Understand the different types of AI and how they are applied
- Understand Google's contribution to the space of AI
- Understand the considerations that are required when preparing to leverage AI
- Describe the Google Cloud solutions for ML and AI

The chapter covers the following topics:

- AI overview and Google's contribution
- Considerations when building AI models
- Google Cloud solutions for ML and AI

AI overview and Google's contribution

Google has made meaningful contributions in several areas of the ML and AI space. At a high level, Google has been doing research and development in the ML space for a long time, where they've developed frameworks such as **TensorFlow**, which makes it easier to train ML models. Google also has an extensive library of models that they developed themselves, which can be applied across a variety of data and use cases. One of the most impactful projects in the natural language processing space was the development of the **Transformer architecture**, the foundation upon which the generative AI revolution was built. What's interesting about the Transformer architecture is that it is based on the self-attention mechanism, where the model can learn the relationship between words in a sequence without relying on the order of the words. We'll dive deeper into generative AI models and applications later in this chapter, but it's important to highlight how the *T* in **ChatGPT** stands for Transformer, which was ultimately a Google development dating back to 2017.

Within the space of Google Search, they've been leveraging ML models for over a decade to help understand the intent behind a query and surface the most relevant information. Within the world of Google Ads, they've been using ML to empower clients with capabilities such as smart bidding, allowing them to optimize their bidding strategy based on their desired goals, such as maximizing clicks, conversions, or return on ad spend.

Much of this work comes from Google's AI research divisions, which were recently merged. **Google Research** and **DeepMind** were two different organizations within Alphabet that were tasked with conducting research in advanced technologies and exploring their applications. DeepMind is particularly famous for its model, known as **AlphaGo**, which was trained to specifically play the game Go and was able to defeat a top global player, Lee Sedol, back in 2016. This project served as a proof of concept that ML models were not only able to compete with but defeat top-ranked players. Go had been thought of as a deeply complex and ancient game that was beyond the scope of machines to fully understand and play at a high level. By defeating a top player in a 5-match series, the DeepMind team proved ML systems could go toe to toe with human beings, even in advanced and complex tasks.

Recently, DeepMind and Google Research were merged to form **Google DeepMind**, an effort to align both organizations to Google's and Alphabet's strategic goals for AI. This move is proving to be significant in accelerating Google's ability to build models and launch them for external usage, something that we'll explore later in this chapter as it relates to the recent launches for generative AI.

How AI and ML models can be applied across industries varies widely based on the types of data that are available and what outcome is being driven. From a 10,000-foot view, there are a few categories of ML models based on data type – natural language processing, image/video processing, speech processing, and structured data models. Natural language models are models that are built and designed to help analyze text at scale. They might execute tasks such as translating text from one language into another, summarizing a large body of text, answering a question, or even analyzing the emotional sentiment of a set of texts. Use cases for these kinds of models include natural language query engines, chatbots, and customer sentiment analysis.

Image and video models focus more on analyzing the content embedded in an image or series of images. These kinds of models are used to scrape data from files such as scanned documents or PDFs and land it in a data warehouse, for example, to facilitate the digitization of assets and analysis of the content. Assuming there is no need to scrape data from a file and the use case has more to do with analyzing the image or video itself, models can identify specific objects with the image or video feed to trigger specific outcomes or workflows. An example of this is having a motion detection algorithm running on a security camera and doing object detection whenever the motion is detected. This can be used to send alerts – for example, when the mail person drops a package off at a home. You can also scrape specific data points from videos, where for example a parking lot may capture the license plate of a delivery vehicle for inventory management purposes.

Voice models focus on recognizing the spoken language and transcription. These models are great for capturing information that may not be available in written format. They often output text transcriptions that can then be used for analytics and the natural language processing that we covered earlier in this chapter. An interesting way that this technology is applied is in live translation. If you can transcribe, in real time, what is being said, you can also translate it to make the content more accessible to people around the world.

Voice, natural language processing, image, and video analysis are more modern applications of ML models. Many of the ML models that are used today focus on solving problems such as demand forecasting, route optimization, or recommendations. These models are for solving structured data problems and can also be incredibly useful. For example, an e-commerce company may be trying to understand its customer base and buying patterns more thoroughly. This may mean doing things such as lifetime value analysis and recommending products based on historical purchasing patterns of other, similar customers.

ML, more broadly, refers to the ability to have machines write code for themselves to understand the data being fed to them and what output is required. Historically, the way machines were programmed was by having a person script specific instructions for the machine to follow. In some circumstances, however, it can be very difficult or even impossible to code your way through a problem. For example, imagine having to write a program that differentiates between a Yorkshire terrier and a cat of a similar color. How would you describe the difference? One is a dog and the other is a cat, but what fundamentally differentiates the two? What ML researchers found was that instead of trying to write code that will be able to define and differentiate between both, you can just feed an ML model examples of a cat and examples of a Yorkie. The model can then define for itself what it finds to be meaningful differences between the two and provide an output based on this analysis. The model would essentially predict with a certain level of accuracy and confidence whether new images are of a cat or a dog.

The preceding example is a great demonstration of how an image classification model can be applied. Classification is one of the core use cases for ML models across all of the modalities, which include text, image, and video.

Forecasting is another great example of how ML models for structured data can be applied. You can feed an ML model a dataset with historical sales data and then use it to predict future sales. This kind of forecasting can be really powerful to identify areas where the business may be struggling, or the forecasting suggests may be at risk, and empower folks to take action. If your forecast within a geographic area is low, perhaps it would make sense to run a targeted marketing campaign for that specific market. Perhaps an internal investigation may make sense to understand why that specific market is struggling. Are you pushing campaigns for football teams that aren't relevant to that market? A campaign related to American football, for example, may see significant success in the United States, but a campaign focused on soccer may be more relevant for European, African, or South American markets.

The latest revolution in the ML and AI space has been the public availability of large language and generative AI models. **Large language models (LLMs)** are models that are trained by being fed large volumes of text. These models can understand natural language and provide responses in a natural language given the dataset that they were trained on. Generative AI is a class of ML models that focuses on generating content. They can generate summaries based on a large body of text, do the inverse, or even generate images.

You can almost think of LLMs as advanced prediction models where instead of predicting the next word in a sentence or how to finish a sentence, they understand the intent of a question and generate a structured response in natural language. This reduces the barrier of entry when using technology because where people historically would've had to know the SQL query language to interact with a database or be familiar with how to optimize a search based on keywords, they can provide guidance to a model and have it generate valuable output.

Some examples of how this technology is being applied in the consumer space with Google's **Bard**, their proprietary LLM-based, general chatbot, is to generate templates for blog posts, provide travel itineraries based on specific cities, and answer general questions.

Something to keep in mind with generative models is that they are prone to something called **hallucination**. Generative AI models are chaotic by definition, in that they have been trained on a very large corpus of data and sometimes, the connections that it makes may cause it to generate content that is not accurate. This is something that can be tuned and restrained through strategies such as constraining the model to responses from a specific corpus of data and forcing it to cite sources, a technique called grounding. Another technique for manipulating model responses is prompt engineering. Prompt engineering refers to changing the prompt for the LLM in the hopes of eliciting a specific kind of response.

An example of hallucination would be if an LLM chatbot is trained to provide a specific output – let's say a structured response – to describe the life and works of an author. Assuming that it can't find enough information about a specific author to complete the template, the model may fabricate information to ensure it complies with the output structure or even use information from a completely different author. It will be great at providing a response that *looks* right based on the output but the information within the output can be completely erroneous or nonsensical.

While Bard is Google's consumer-facing product, they are also making enterprise-grade models and platforms for folks who want to leverage Google's technologies within their companies or applications. We'll dive deeper into what is available in the Google Cloud platform later, but it's good to highlight at this point that when it comes to corporate use cases, customers should be using the Vertex AI platform and PaLM models through Google Cloud rather than Bard. **Vertex AI** is a serverless, full life cycle model management platform that folks can use to train, tune, deploy, and manage their models. It helps establish a level of operational rigor for organizations as it is built to enable **ML operations (MLOps)** practices, a field that Google is pioneering similar to DevOps and SRE. **PaLM** is Google's LLM that is powering the different APIs in Google Cloud for addressing generative AI use cases. Google has also teased the launch of **Gemini**, the next-generation model for LLM and generative AI use cases that will be released soon.

Now that we've explored some of the different kinds of models that can be trained and the use cases where they apply, let's explore what considerations are required when kicking off an ML project.

Considerations when building AI models

One of the most important adages of the ML space is *garbage in, garbage out*. This refers to the fact that if you feed a model data that is not representative of production data, the model will likely not be very accurate or useful. This is important to keep in mind as the instinct may be to feed a model as much data as possible to train the best model. However, when you have trained a massive model, it's not very cost-effective to serve in production. As you can imagine, the more data you feed a model, the more it'll cost to train and the larger the model will be when it needs to be served in production. Therefore, in the world of ML, although the first iteration of a model may be based on a larger dataset, future iterations will try to strip away data that doesn't improve the quality of the model to condense the model into its most cost-effective version. This technique is known as feature engineering. Ideally, this model can eventually be pushed to the edge so that you can offload the compute work of predictions to the edge device, such as a smartphone or a laptop. This minimizes latency, given that there would be no internet connection required to serve the model and provide the optimal client experience.

Defining the problem

There are several considerations when preparing to build an ML model. One of the most important is to start with a problem that you are trying to solve. Technology for technology's sake often ends up becoming a science project that doesn't get adopted in a meaningful way by the business or customers. Does the business have an issue, is it inefficient at something, or is there some function that is cost-prohibitive? Where is the customer experiencing pain? Are you trying to predict, classify, or cluster something?

Collecting the datasets

Once the problem that is to be resolved is defined, it's time to collect datasets. Ideally, the data would be representative of the real-world data that the model would be served. This may mean exporting historical data from internal systems such as data from point of sale systems, customer relationship management systems, marketing, and customer survey data. Just collecting the data, however, is not enough.

Preparing the data

You will need to ensure the data is properly prepared by cleaning it. This may entail removing outliers, which tend to skew data, and normalizing it to ensure it is consistent. Collecting several datasets and merging them is valuable because it allows you and the model to derive value and insights that may not be obvious at face value. For example, if you are an e-commerce firm that sells clothing apparel, you may choose to enrich your dataset with weather data to have the model take into account the weather forecast for the week to optimize your product recommendations. If it's supposed to rain, running a campaign for rain boots and raincoats could be more successful than running a normal campaign for shirts or pants.

Select the model and train it

Now that you've defined what datasets are available and prepared the data for training, it's time to define a model and approach. Many different ML algorithms can be useful, depending on the circumstances. **Clustering models**, for example, can be great for providing product or music recommendations. A **time series prediction model** would be great for forecasting sales based on historical data. The data type that's available and the target outcome will guide you to which model makes sense. If multiple models are relevant, you may weave multiple models together to drive toward a specific workflow or outcome. Model training may take time, depending on the size of the dataset and the infrastructure available for training. A technical team may also implement engineering-driven optimization to improve the quality of the training and the model. This includes feature engineering, where you seek to strip away noisy data that doesn't meaningfully influence the inference, and hyperparameter tuning, where the training parameters are adjusted to elicit a specific type of response.

Evaluating the model

Congratulations! You've trained an ML model, but is it any good? Once a model has been trained, it's important to test its efficacy against a portion of the dataset that was collected but not used to train the model. To truly evaluate its performance, you must serve the model data upon which it was not trained, similar to what it would see in the real world or production. This will inform you whether you have something usable. Assuming the model does not perform well, you may need to do additional training or more finely curate the dataset being used to train the model. Feeding a model repeat data can reduce its accuracy and confidence, and therefore its usability.

Deploying the model

Assuming your model was trained on enough clean data and can pass the testing and validation phase, the next step is to deploy the model in production. Models are often packaged in containers and served through API calls. The beauty of containers and Kubernetes running the model is that you can scale the ability to serve requests based on load. We'll dive deeper into Kubernetes and containers in the infrastructure section of this book, but it's important to note that the work does not finish once a model is ready for production – there are infrastructure considerations when pushing things to production.

Monitoring the model

Once the model is being served in production, it's important to monitor the health and accuracy of the model. There is the potential for model quality to degrade over time as data evolves and behavior changes. You may need to periodically retain the model on more recent data or you may need a new model to take into account new datasets or changes in customer purchasing patterns. A great example of this is the difference in purchasing patterns during COVID-19 lockdowns and after the world reopened. If you had built and launched a product recommendation engine during COVID-19 for home furnishings, you might have been recommending things such as stand-up desks, computer chairs, and associated electronics. Now that the world is open again, perhaps consumer behavior has changed, and folks are starting to focus more on furnishings that can be used in group activities such as couches and dining tables.

Beyond technical considerations, there are also human factors that need to be taken into account when preparing for ML projects. You may need to rally internal and external stakeholders to support the effort, given that it could require resources such as internal headcount and external customer data. You also need to build a team that can move quickly and iterate on learnings along the journey. You'll need input from someone on the business side of the company to define a meaningful problem and you'll need help from project management resources to help define the scope of the project and timelines for deliverables. You'll also need to bring together folks with technical expertise and experience that complement each other. For example, an AI tiger team may consist of a cloud engineer to provision the development environment and permissions, a data engineer to collect and consolidate the datasets, and an ML engineer or data scientist to inform on the modeling approach. Once a model has been trained, you'll likely need to coordinate with the infrastructure team to have it deployed. This may mean partnering with the DevOps team to build out infrastructure to serve the model and monitor the health of the infrastructure itself.

Now that we have a high-level understanding of how folks should approach AI projects, we're ready to dive into the Google Cloud solutions that are available for AI and ML.

Google Cloud solutions for ML and AI

Google Cloud provides a broad range of solutions to help folks leverage AI regardless of where they are in their data maturity journey. If you are a business user who wants to have a model autocomplete your words and sentences, Gmail or Google Docs may be very valuable. If, however, you are building applications and want to embed AI capabilities within your application, that's where the Vertex AI platform truly shines.

There are essentially three ways to use ML models on Google Cloud: leverage off-the-shelf models, customize off-the-shelf models with your data and use case, or build models from scratch.

Pre-built models include models for natural language processing, image processing, and structured data processing such as clustering and linear regression. Google also provides the ability to tailor these pretrained models to your use case by training them on your data and classifiers. This is great when one of the pretrained models can't quite handle your use case but are relatively close. Assuming customizing a Google model to your use case still doesn't provide the outcome that is needed, customers can also leverage the platform and tooling to build models from scratch. Training models from the ground up tends to be more time-consuming and requires more data. Generally speaking, you need 10,000 examples of something to have a statistically significant dataset and that is typically the order of magnitude required for training a model from the ground up. What's great about using Google's tuning approach, where you customize an existing, trained model, is that you start with an already high-quality model that needs an order of magnitude less data to be specialized to a new use case. Think about teaching a child to recite a poem. If the child already speaks English and knows how to read, you'll be able to build on that knowledge to get them to quickly recite the poem accurately. However, if the child doesn't speak English and can't read, you'll have to spend significantly more time preparing them.

Vertex AI and its associated services

Let's go ahead and explore the core services available for ML development and life cycle management on Google Cloud, starting with the overall platform and highlighting some of its key features and capabilities.

Vertex AI

Let's explore Vertex AI:

- **Description**: A serverless platform to facilitate ML model training, iteration, deployment, and full life cycle management. Vertex includes several components, such as the model garden and workbench.

- **Use case**: An end-to-end model management platform to help implement MLOps practices to efficiently manage, monitor, and govern ML models and workloads.

- **Competitors**: MLFlow, Azure Machine Learning, and SageMaker.

TensorFlow processing units (TPUs)

Let's explore TPUs:

- **Description**: ML-focused processing units that are designed to be suited for large matrix operations such as training deep neural network models. They are very efficient from a power consumption perspective, making them very attractive from a cost perspective relative to other processing units.

- **Use case**: Training deep neural networks, speed, and cost-effectiveness.

Vertex AI Model Garden

Let's explore Vertex AI Model Garden:

- **Description**: A catalog of first-party, open source, and third-party ML models that makes it easy to explore and test models and APIs

- **Use case**: Model exploration and evaluation

Vertex AI Pipelines

Let's explore the Vertex AI Pipelines:

- **Description**: A serverless pipeline service that helps with the automation, monitoring, and governance of ML pipelines, a component of MLOps

- **Use case**: Data pipeline orchestration, optimized for ML model development

Vertex ML Model Registry

Let's explore Vertex ML Model Registry:

- **Description**: A service that helps catalog, track, and manage ML models and their lineages, a component of MLOps

- **Use case**: Model repository and catalog

AutoML

Let's explore AutoML:

- **Description**: A serverless service for tuning existing ML models to specific data and use cases with minimal effort and ML experience

- **Use case**: Building custom ML models

BigQuery ML

Let's explore BigQuery ML:

- **Description**: It allows you to run ML models and train customer ML models using standard SQL on your data residing in BigQuery with native platform functionality
- **Use case**: Training structured data models and running inference on data without having to build pipelines

Let's go beyond the Vertex AI platform and explore the different ML APIs available through Google Cloud.

ML APIs

Beyond the specific services shared previously, Google also makes easy-to-use ML APIs available that can help with specific tasks. For example, the translation API can translate text into different, supported languages. Let's go ahead and provide a summary of the available APIs.

Natural language processing

Let's explore natural language processing:

- **Description**: Analyze and extract value from text
- **Use case**: Natural language understanding for classification, extraction, and sentiment

Speech-to-text

Let's explore speech-to-text:

- **Description**: Understands the spoken language and converts it into text
- **Use case**: Speech recognition and transcription

Text-to-speech

Let's explore text-to-speech:

- **Description**: Able to generate spoken language from a text file
- **Use case**: Voice-activated customer experiences

Vision AI

Let's explore Vision AI:

- **Description**: Analyze and extract insights from images
- **Use case**: Derive insights from images such as object detection and text extraction

Video AI

Let's explore Video AI:

- **Description**: Analyze and extract insights from videos
- **Use case**: Create and extract relevant metadata from the video down to specific frames, as well as identify entities within videos

Let's move on to the next solution.

AI business solutions

In addition to the Vertex AI platform, its associated services, and ML APIs, Google Cloud has also started venturing into the world of building solutions for clients. While Vertex could be considered a solution for building ML models, it's not a solution in and of itself. It's a platform tool that folks can use to build, maintain, and iterate on ML models.

There are a few solutions that weave together some of the preceding services and offerings to provide something more holistic for clients. Let's go ahead and explore them.

Contact Center AI (CCAI)

Let's explore CCAI:

- **Description**: The CCAI solution weaves together different technologies such as chatbots and natural language processing models to help clients create advanced virtual agents
- **Use case**: Personalized customer care powered by AI working in tandem with humans across multiple channels

Document AI (DocAI)

Let's explore DocAI:

- **Description**: DocAI allows clients to easily extract entities from documents and make them easily searchable
- **Use case**: Document digitization, as well as entity extraction and search

Product discovery

Let's explore product discovery:

- **Description**: It provides product search and recommendations that are personalized based on improving the shopper experience and maximizing shopper conversion
- **Use case**: Natural language search, image-based search, and personalization

These solutions are great for folks who have a specific outcome in mind, such as embedding Google-grade search into an eCommerce storefront or building a dynamic, conversational agent to help with customer support flows.

Generative AI

We've now covered the core of what's available for Google Cloud as far as traditional ML goes. The latest wave of innovation in 2023 has been centered around LLMs. These models, as mentioned previously, are more dynamic in understanding human language and the intent behind it and can provide outputs that are also more dynamic.

Generative AI models range from models focused on question and answer to dynamic interactions such as conversations, image generation, and even code completion. Google has released several foundation models upon which its offerings are built. Some examples are PaLM for conversational AI and natural language understanding, **Imagen** for image generation based on text descriptions, and **Codey** for code completion and autocorrect.

These models are being woven into existing Google technology such as Google Workspace, where you can ask PaLM to generate a template for a blog post, for example, directly from Google Docs, while Imagen is available through Google Slides, where you can ask it to generate a specific image for you. Through Google Cloud and Vertex AI, Google is also making these foundation models available to developers who can then build them into their applications. Let's explore the infrastructure offerings, foundation models, and solutions a bit deeper.

PaLM for text

Let's explore PaLM for text:

- **Description**: An LLM that's well suited to text-based use cases
- **Use case**: This model is ideal for tasks such as summarization and extrapolation

PaLM for chat

Let's explore PaLM for chat:

- **Description**: Multi-turn conversational interactions that can build off of session context
- **Use case**: Support workflows and multiple questions and answers that are interconnected

Chirp for speech

Let's explore Chirp for speech:

- **Description**: A universal speech model that can understand multiple languages and convert speech into text
- **Use case**: Speech recognition and transcription; it supports multiple languages

Imagen for text to image

Let's explore Imagen for text to image:

- **Description**: A text-to-image generation model that creates image content based on a description
- **Use case**: Content and image generation

The embeddings API for text to image

Let's explore the embeddings API for text to image:

- **Description**: This is a service that allows for the creation and management of embeddings, which are vector representations of data such as the meaning of words and phrases
- **Use case**: Sentiment analysis, classification, and recommendations

Codey

Let's explore Codey:

- **Description**: A code generation model that helps improve coding and debugging
- **Use case**: Code autocomplete and autocorrect

Google AI Studio

Let's explore Google AI Studio:

- **Description**: A developer-centric experience that abstracts away much of the complexity of building and managing ML models by focusing on designing a specific workflow or solution such as chatbots or search engines
- **Use case**: Quickly and easily build applications with out-of-the-box capabilities around conversational AI, conversational search, and chatbots

Gemini

Let's explore Gemini:

- **Description**: This is Google's latest GenAI foundation model family. It's built to be natively multi-modal, being able to handle multiple inputs such as text, images, and video. Gemini is offered in a few different versions:

  - **Nano**: For on-device tasks such as running on a Pixel smartphone

  - **Pro**: A flexible and general cloud-based model that is great for scaling across a variety of tasks

  - **Ultra**: The largest and most capable model for highly complex tasks

- **Use case**: Quickly and easily build applications with out-of-the-box capabilities around conversational AI, conversational search, and chatbots.

> **Note**
>
> All of this may seem a bit overwhelming, especially if you are new to ML or ML on Google Cloud. However, remember that the exam – depending on when you take it – may not cover the generative AI content very deeply, so focusing on Vertex and its value, as well as the APIs and solutions, will likely be enough to pass the exam.

When building a solution that leverages AI, it's important to keep in mind that the focus should be on the experience that needs to be delivered to the customer. AI is a tool just like any other tool – it is useful when applied correctly. Often, developers will end up weaving together a symphony of models to deliver a specific customer experience.

Summary

Google has made considerable contributions to the field of ML and many of the capabilities being launched through Google Cloud are an extension of this work. Where the Google Research or DeepMind teams might've historically shared their research exclusively through research papers and eventually open source projects, they can now deliver capabilities directly to Google Cloud customers through the Vertex AI platform and other associated services.

Whether you have a structured data problem to be solved with ML or just need to scrape the information that resides in scanned document files, you will likely find a service or set of services that can help on Google Cloud. Not only does Google Cloud have an extremely robust offering for its infrastructure, foundation models, and APIs, but it also has an extremely mature security posture, which allows it to deliver best-in-class security for any work being done on Google Cloud. In the next section of this book, we'll explore Google Cloud's compute infrastructure offerings while also touching on the ever-important topic of security.

Part 3: Infrastructure and Platform Modernization

The third part of this book will cover infrastructure and application modernization with Google Cloud. This includes highlighting the differences between legacy and cloud-native applications, the value of a cloud-native approach, and how APIs can be leveraged to modernize legacy applications.

This part has the following chapters:

7

Modernizing IT Infrastructure with Google Cloud

Part 3 of this book will focus on the infrastructure component of cloud systems as we explore the different hosting services and best practices for cloud operations. *Chapter 7* in particular will focus on the evolution of IT infrastructure. We'll dig into the challenges associated with running traditional systems and why they struggle in the modern world. We'll also highlight the value of modernizing infrastructure with cloud technologies, the differences between hybrid and multi-cloud, and navigate the evolution of computing from mainframes to **virtual machines** (**VMs**) to containers.

By the end of this chapter, you will be able to do the following:

- Explain how the evolution of customer needs causes challenges for legacy infrastructure
- Describe the advantages of cloud technologies and modernizing infrastructure
- Compare and contrast virtualization, containerization, and serverless

The chapter covers the following topics:

- The challenges with legacy infrastructure in the modern world
- The value of modernizing infrastructure with cloud technologies
- The differences between hybrid and multi-cloud
- The evolution of computing from VMs to containers to serverless

The challenges with legacy infrastructure in the modern world

In an increasingly interconnected, globalized world, organizations have had to transform themselves to service their customers, battle competitors, and continue to grow. Firms who might've thought of themselves as regional or national players began to understand that expanding beyond their region or nation was becoming more cost-effective, safe, and practical. Opening up a new market such as Europe, South America, or Asia provided the opportunity to service hundreds of millions of new customers while also introducing complexity to the business.

For a manufacturing company, this may mean continuing to manufacture a product domestically while shipping it overseas. However, what if your product is not price-competitive in certain markets due to the labor cost of your domestic market? For some folks, it may make more sense to spin up manufacturing capacity in India or South America to specifically serve those markets. The plant would be able to be built more cost-effectively in those markets and the lower labor costs could offset the price disparity between a foreign product and its local competitors. Effectively, the complexity that had to be overcome to take advantage of a global market included navigating language barriers, engaging with foreign governments, and developing new supply and distribution chains.

This shift to a global mindset of doing business also had an impact on how companies designed, deployed, and managed systems. The traditional approach to infrastructure was to establish regional data centers or concentrations of compute power to minimize the cost of procuring and running infrastructure. By centralizing infrastructure, you can make large capital investments more efficient by procuring land, hardware, and software in bulk.

The paradox, however, is that users tend to be in areas that are densely populated, and in areas of dense population, the cost of land tends to be proportionally high. Therefore, there is a constant tension between performance and cost. Building a data center closer to a large city would produce a better experience for customers but it would also come at a higher cost.

In addition to this paradox, organizations may need to think about regulatory challenges. For example, with the GDPR, **personally identifiable information (PII)** for European citizens needs to be encrypted and ideally hosted within Europe. Some nations may even require that data for their citizens be specifically hosted within their internationally recognized boundaries.

Similar to how the manufacturing sector adopted different practices to compete and grow in a globalized world, the technology space also evolved its technologies and practices over the past few decades. Where mainframes used to dominate the data center, these days, hardware can be pooled and shared across multiple applications thanks to technologies such as virtualization and containerization.

The traditional data center was essentially a regional warehouse where computing resources were centralized to facilitate the procurement, management, and security of those systems. They would have specialized power, cooling, and networking capabilities to serve the systems deployed at the location. If these systems were to be made available over the internet, little thought was dedicated to the **user experience (UX)**. This isn't to say that UX wasn't important but computing was typically used in highly specialized tasks such as running a large database or an order management system, where the integrity of the data was more important than the experience of using the software.

While this centralized, mainframe-based architecture makes sense – where a set of hardware is built out and allocated to a specific application – many applications don't require a massive amount of computing dedicated to it to run. This mainframe-focused data center was very inefficient in its resource usage. While the application may need 80%+ of the hardware to process requests at peak load, what if it only saw peak loads for a couple of hours a month or even just a couple of days a year?

The challenge that virtualization helped overcome in the world of mainframes is that you were able to dissect and allocate virtual resources tied to a physical server across multiple applications. Rather than being married to the concept of one operating system and application per server, with the advent of virtualization, you were able to generate multiple virtual servers from a single, large, physical server, which significantly improved hardware utilization and therefore lowered the cost of running infrastructure.

If you need to run 10 applications, in the world before virtualization, you would essentially need 10 servers and the accompanying licensing to run the applications. As you can imagine, much of the hardware dedicated to those 10 applications may not be in use. Let's go ahead and explore an Acme use case to help you understand the technology purchasing process.

Acme Inc. – buying servers

You are the director of infrastructure at a financial organization and you've been tasked with building a small data center. Your company has started digitizing processes, so you need a set of applications deployed within your organization to leverage this new digital way of doing business. You meet with your systems team to map out the hardware requirements. Some of the applications require operating system X, while others require operating system Y. You also review the hardware requirements for the applications to ensure they won't underperform once they're deployed. Your team has not adopted virtualization yet, so you need to acquire hardware that's specific to each application.

Based on your exploration, you define that you need five servers with 6 cores and 10 GB of RAM while for the other five servers, you need 10 cores and 14 GB of RAM. With these requirements, you can now go to a technology reseller and procure the hardware. You share your requirements with the reseller and they provide you with a few quotes. There are just a few issues that need to be addressed:

- The reseller and their manufacturers do not offer servers with six or 10 cores; you must choose between 4-core, 8-core, or 12-core servers

- The reseller and their manufacturers do not offer servers with 14 GB of RAM unless you purchase a server with a minimum of 12 cores

To meet the needs of the applications you'll be supporting, the team procures more hardware than is required, but it's justified by the fact that the server vendors offer specific sizing for servers and that you would have some room to grow if needed. You end up procuring five servers with 8 cores and 10 GB of RAM and four servers with 12 cores and 14 GB of RAM. Let's review this:

Requirement	Availability	Cost/Server	Quantity	Total Cost
6 cores/10 GB of RAM	8 cores/10 GB of RAM	$5,000	5	$25,000
10 cores/14 GB of RAM	12 cores/14 GB of RAM	$7,500	5	$37,500

Table 7.1 – Hardware procurement for individual servers

Now, let's look at the cost of being over-provisioned before exploring the virtualization use case. Given that the reseller only had specific sizing for servers, you were forced to overprovision two cores per server across all 10 servers. This means that 20 of the 80 cores you've procured – or 25% of your CPU capacity – would be wasted based on the requirements of the applications.

This is an example of how hardware requirements for an application do not always align with the procurement process based on how server manufacturers build and size their contracts. The issue is that technology projects tend to be very sizable and can ramp aggressively over time, depending on the circumstances.

Imagine the amount of hardware waste in a data center that procured 100 servers, 1,000 servers, or even 10,000 servers. At scale, hardware underutilization becomes a big issue as wasted capacity can account for thousands if not millions of procurement dollars that go to waste. This waste is composed of maintenance costs, utility costs, low utilization of headcount, and unused software costs among other inefficient allocations of resources.

Virtualization was developed to help overcome this challenge and increase hardware utilization. Virtualization software is software that creates the ability to virtually allocate portions of a server's hardware to multiple VMs that can run different operating systems and applications. For example, instead of purchasing 10 servers to run 10 different applications, you would be able to purchase one very large server, install virtualization software on it, and then carve up portions of its hardware to be dedicated to specific applications.

Now, let's explore the procurement scenario for a server that can be virtualized.

You meet with the team and the hardware requirements for the applications are the same but you can pool the resources for procurement. Rather than purchasing 10 individual servers with some variation in requirements, you can reach out to a reseller with a total requirement of cores and purchase it in bulk. This is what it would look like for a procurement request:

Requirement	Cost
80 cores/120 GB of RAM	$50,000

Table 7.2 – Hardware procurement for pooled hardware

By pooling together all of the resources, a hardware procurement team can overcome some of the challenges around server sizing while also getting a lower cost for the overall order. The preceding examples are meant to be illustrative and shouldn't be regarded as accurate cost scenarios, but it's helpful to showcase the purchasing process for technology and some of the considerations when making a purchasing decision.

Other than cost and utilization, there are several other reasons that legacy infrastructure can struggle to serve the needs of modern customers:

- Outdated hardware or software
- Lack of scalability and flexibility
- Security vulnerabilities
- High maintenance costs

Let us look at these in some detail:

Outdated hardware or software

Outdated hardware and software can become big issues for organizations as they manage technology infrastructure at scale. In some circumstances, a specific system or application may have an operating system dependency, for example, and only be functional on software that is no longer supported by the manufacturer. This means that any issues with the legacy systems may be very difficult to address or be outside the scope of the terms of service with the manufacturer. This means that bugs or patches that are required to keep the software secure and performant will not be developed. These systems may also struggle to integrate with other, more modern systems, which may be required for advanced projects such as real-time data pipelines or machine learning.

Lack of scalability and flexibility

Working with legacy systems also surfaces challenges around scalability and flexibility. Where modern systems are built on top of containers and Kubernetes, being able to gracefully scale up and down based on load, legacy systems are typically server-centric and therefore coupled with the underlying hardware. These systems tend to be monolithic, having an application whose code base is interconnected across all or most of its functions, making it very difficult to make changes, update, and scale it. These systems are not very flexible, tend to have very specific technical requirements to function, and may not be equipped to integrate with other, modern systems.

Security vulnerabilities

Security vulnerabilities are a big challenge to manage with legacy systems, particularly when systems are no longer supported by the manufacturer. Similar to bugs, manufacturers will not support building and launching security patches for legacy operating systems and applications. This means that any new vulnerabilities found in the code will be perpetual, with no prospect of having it directly addressed through changes to the code base. Attackers will know which vulnerabilities have been identified and will look to exploit those vulnerabilities. These systems will have also been designed without taking into account the latest evolutions of the security space, such as zero-trust security. This would mean that they may not be able to support things such as multi-factor authentication, which are now considered to be best practices for any secure, enterprise-grade system.

High maintenance costs

Lastly, the cost of maintaining legacy systems can become a big challenge for serving modern use cases and customers. These systems may require specialized hardware and software, which is often sold at a premium, particularly if there's a limited supply. Hiring and retaining talent to manage these systems can also be challenging as they require specialized skill sets that may not be readily available to the broader market. These systems have also been designed and architected without modern best practices around reliability, which can make them prone to failures and performance issues, particularly when trying to handle global traffic or more generally spikes in traffic. This can have adverse impacts on customers, especially if the application is tied to something that's externally-facing and mission-critical for a business.

Having explored some of the challenges associated with serving customers on legacy systems, let's explore the advantages of modernizing legacy systems by leveraging cloud-native practices and technologies.

The value of modernizing infrastructure with cloud technologies

The traditional approach to managing applications and their infrastructure is to treat each application as a unique system that needs to be tended to on an individual level. Each server was sized to meet the individual needs of an application and a lot of time was dedicated to servicing them. With the shift to the cloud, where the management of the underlying hardware could be abstracted away from infrastructure teams, the mentality around managing technology systems has shifted from managing the individual server to treating servers like a herd and managing the herd at scale.

This approach allows technology teams to be much more efficient with their headcount and skills development, given that work that would normally be the full-time job of an engineer is offloaded to code and automation. Rather than having an engineering team provision 100 physical servers for a specific project, which can take months depending on hardware availability and the procurement process, one engineer can spin up 100 virtual servers in a third party's data center and ensure this via a web portal.

Beyond the ability to provision infrastructure from the web, which saves a lot of time and money – particularly when having to troubleshoot data center issues – these systems are treated as a herd and managed at scale through technologies such as containerization and container orchestration services such as Kubernetes.

We'll dig deeper into containers and serverless later in this chapter to describe why cloud systems can be built and managed through automation. However, we'll start by exploring the reasons why cloud infrastructure benefits businesses:

- Agility
- Scalability
- Resilience
- Security

Let us look at these in detail.

Agility

When deploying systems through a cloud infrastructure provider, organizations can bypass many of the challenges associated with building infrastructure, such as hardware availability, time to value, and complexity. If a developer team is throttled in its ability to build applications and launch them to users, it'll take a significant amount of time to be able to iterate on the solution that they are developing. A technology company's ability to ship code is correlated with its ability to launch new features and applications and fix issues such as bugs. If it takes a developer a week, a month, or several months to have hardware provisioned for them to deploy their applications, their productivity will be impacted. In the world of cloud infrastructure, all that a cloud engineer has to do to provision hardware is click a few buttons or issue some commands. The beauty is that the cloud vendor takes on the responsibilities around hardware availability across different regions and teams can focus and prioritize their engineering productivity rather than having to navigate complex purchasing processes.

Scalability

Another big advantage of the herd mentality for managing technology systems is that they become much more scalable. Rather than building individual servers that require unique hardware or software, organizations had to treat hardware as a commodity and code. They can build scripts to quickly deploy one, 10, or 100 servers and even dynamically scale the infrastructure based on load. This also makes it easier to scale a company globally given that you wouldn't have to navigate the complexities of building out data center capacity in countries where an organization may have little knowledge of how to execute a large, physical, and capital-intensive project. Within Google Cloud, engineers can quickly and easily spin up servers across multiple regions scattered all over the world and have them communicate through secure connections with minimal time and effort.

Resilience

Resilience is another meaningful benefit of leveraging cloud infrastructure. Engineers can architect systems to be fault-tolerant across multiple geographies or even platforms. For example, a Google Cloud customer can manage and secure Kubernetes workloads across AWS, Azure, Google Cloud, and on-premises environments, allowing for highly resilient and reliable systems that have fault tolerance built in and even the ability to fail over to multiple environments depending on the circumstances. This resilience can be deeply meaningful to organizations such as those in the financial services sector, where any downtime can be considered disruptive and negatively impact the customer experience.

Security

Last but not least, leveraging cloud infrastructure can help improve an organization's security posture. In the world of on-premises or collocations, the customer engineering team is responsible for securing the environment at every level of the stack. This means that folks have to build specific teams and competence around designing, building, and maintaining secure systems from physical security to hardware to operating systems and applications. When working with cloud infrastructure, the vendors themselves take on a meaningful portion of the work for security technology systems. Depending on the type of cloud service, the provider will be responsible for the underlying security of systems and can even take on additional roles by providing technologies that are natively built to secure their platform. With Google Cloud, for example, you can leverage technologies such as Cloud Armor for DDoS attack protection and Cloud Security Command Center to identify issues with configurations that could trigger compliance violations.

While there are many other benefits in addition to the ones listed earlier, such as leveraging innovation from cloud providers, let's explore the difference between hybrid and multi-cloud environments to ensure there's no confusion between the two.

The differences between hybrid and multi-cloud

Whenever a technology team decides to adopt one cloud or multiple cloud infrastructure platforms, these platforms may need to be integrated with other existing systems. Whether there were existing on-premises environments that they wanted to migrate or were already using a different platform, there may be nuances for how to properly connect them to ensure secure communications.

Let's go ahead and clarify the classification for the different terms.

A **hybrid cloud environment** is a cloud computing environment that combines on-premises infrastructure with public cloud services. This allows organizations to keep some of their data and applications on-premises, while others are moved to the public cloud.

Hybrid cloud environments make sense when an organization has already made meaningful investments in its on-premises infrastructure and may not be able to fully migrate all of its infrastructure. There may also be systems that have been deployed within the on-premises infrastructure that have specific hardware dependencies or that need to be on-premises through contractual obligations. In these circumstances, customers will migrate or deploy services that will benefit from the cloud infrastructure and retain their on-premises environment for systems that require it.

A **multi-cloud environment** is a technology ecosystem within a company that uses two or more public cloud infrastructure platforms. This allows organizations to take advantage of the different features and benefits offered by different cloud providers while avoiding issues such as vendor lock-in, where they are at the mercy of one manufacturer and can't negotiate prices based on what other providers are offering.

This may mean stringing together two or more cloud environments to deliver a set of services and capabilities. A customer may choose to leverage Azure for their Microsoft workloads such as Windows servers while using Google Cloud for Linux workloads, containerization, data, and AI.

The main difference between hybrid cloud and multi-cloud environments is the use of on-premises infrastructure. Hybrid cloud environments always include some on-premises infrastructure, while multi-cloud environments do not.

The best cloud computing environment for your organization will depend on your specific needs. If you have sensitive data or applications that need to be kept on-premises, or if you need to comply with specific regulations, then a hybrid cloud environment may be the best option for you. If you want to take advantage of the different features and benefits offered by different cloud providers, or if you want to avoid vendor lock-in, then a multi-cloud environment may be the best option for you.

It is also possible to combine hybrid cloud and multi-cloud environments. For example, an organization could use a hybrid cloud environment for its sensitive data and applications, and a multi-cloud environment for its less sensitive data and applications.

The evolution of computing from VMs to containers to serverless

Earlier in this chapter, we touched on the evolution of computing from mainframes and applications with dedicated servers to VMs, where you can purchase hardware in bulk and allocate portions of it to different applications. This evolution was extremely meaningful as VMware rose to glory and organizations around the world adopted virtualization, making computing more cost-effective.

VMs are software that emulates a physical computer. Each VM has an operating system and resources, such as CPU, memory, and storage. VMs can be used to run any type of application, including web applications, databases, and development environments.

Some of the challenges with virtualization include resource efficiency, agility, scalability, and cost. Because each VM requires an operating system, VMs will require the resources to run a full guest operating system as well as the application, which consumes significant resources. This dependence on the guest operating system for VMs also has a considerable impact on agility and scalability. It may take several minutes for the VM to boot, which can impact how quickly you can scale your infrastructure during peak traffic. Also, depending on an application's dependency on its operating system, there could be additional software costs associated with procuring all of the licenses to run those operating systems and VMs.

Containers, on the other hand, share the operating system and kernel with the host machine, significantly reducing the resource requirements and enabling denser deployments.

Containers are lightweight, portable units of software that contain everything needed to run an application, including the code, runtime, system tools, and system libraries. Containers are isolated from each other, so they do not share resources or interfere with each other. This makes them ideal for running multiple applications on the same server. For example, in the world of VMs, you may be able to carve a server up into 10 VMs and run 10 different applications. By pairing VMs and containers, where you could run 20 containerized workloads per VM, you would be able to support 200 apps and services on the same infrastructure.

Over the last 5+ years, the rise of containers and container orchestration systems such as Kubernetes has truly revolutionized computing. Birthed by Google, Kubernetes is a management system that allows you to treat fleets of noes, pods, and containers as a herd and dynamically scale them based on load. When coupled with containers, it empowers organizations to run globally distributed systems that are highly scalable and reliable.

Where you may have needed large teams distributed across the world managing multiple data centers, much of the work of managing infrastructure can be offloaded to Kubernetes, allowing a lean team to run infrastructure across the globe over the internet with minimal effort.

The development of serverless systems has also been on the rise, where infrastructure management, even at the Kubernetes level, is completely abstracted away, allowing technology teams to focus on application development rather than managing infrastructure.

Serverless systems are a cloud computing execution model where the cloud provider manages the server infrastructure and dynamically allocates resources to applications based on demand. This allows developers to focus on writing code without having to worry about managing servers.

App Engine on Google Cloud is a great example of this, where developers focus on developing code and deploying it on a serverless platform and App Engine handles spinning up the underlying infrastructure and its management for the team. This allows organizations to hire more developers over infrastructure engineers, who can then quickly push out updates such as bug fixes and new features, ensuring that you can compete and often outpace the competition.

Serverless systems are also great for tools and platforms that focus on data workloads where there could be significant and complex infrastructure requirements. Systems that do ingestion, data processing, warehousing, machine learning model training, and prediction would all require underlying hardware and systems to do their jobs.

Each type of system can be appropriate, depending on the circumstances, and organizations should pick the best tool for the job based on the requirements of an application, its architecture, and the skills of the team.

VMs are a good choice for running any type of application, but they are especially well-suited for running legacy applications, applications that require a lot of resources, or are highly sensitive to network latency.

Containers are a good choice for running microservices and other cloud-native applications. They enable a more agile development process, the following of DevOps practices, more efficient operations, and cost-efficiency.

Serverless systems are a good choice for running event-driven applications, such as web applications, mobile backends, and APIs. They are also a good choice for running applications that need to be scaled quickly and easily.

As highlighted in this chapter, there are many different ways that an infrastructure team can run an application. Whether they need large, centralized computing like what you get with mainframes or are trying to run globally distributed, scalable applications, ensuring that you make the right architecture decision will ensure that you get the best cost, performance, and experience rations.

Summary

Technology teams will need to consider many different factors when deciding how to host an application and where to host it. Organizations that have legacy applications or the need to retain some level of on-premises infrastructure may choose to stay on-premises or adopt hybrid cloud environments where they land applications that make sense in cloud environments while retaining their on-premises environments for specific applications.

In other circumstances, where an organization is a mature digital native company that was born in the cloud, they may choose to adopt a multi-cloud approach to infrastructure, where they leverage multiple cloud providers to avoid challenges related to vendor lock-in and access to innovation.

Ultimately, there is no silver bullet for solving infrastructure problems, but organizations will weave together a symphony of services and infrastructure to solve specific business problems and technology challenges. A startup may choose to build everything on serverless systems and open source while a larger, traditional enterprise may continue to use VMs in the cloud for some applications while adopting practices such as DevOps for applications that are global, externally facing, and directly linked to revenue generation.

In the next chapter, we'll explore the Google Cloud solutions for infrastructure modernization, application modernization, and the value of cloud-native applications.

Modernizing Applications with Google Cloud

In the previous chapter, we explored the hardware and infrastructure decisions that technology teams make when building out systems in order to support applications. This chapter will focus on the evolution of application development and the implications of these evolutions. It will include a brief history of application development along with a summary of the Google Cloud solutions for hosting applications. After finishing this chapter, you will be able to do the following:

- Understand how and why application development evolved from a monolithic approach to a microservice approach
- Describe the benefits of cloud-native application development and its business drivers
- Describe the solutions available on Google Cloud for hosting applications and when they are appropriate

The chapter covers the following topics:

- The evolution of application development
- The benefits of cloud-native application development
- Google Cloud solutions for hosting applications

The evolution of application development

Application development began as a physical job where punch cards were used to define programming for machines. In particular, the **Electrical Numerical Integrator and Computer** (**ENIC**) machine was invented at the University of Pennsylvania by John W. Mauchly and J. Presper Eckert and was operated by punch card input and outputs. ENIC was also reprogrammable by rewiring the computing machine (https://www.cs.utexas.edu/~mitra/csFall2006/cs303/lectures/history.html).

These punch cards would have holes in them to designate specific instructions, such as running a calculation on a data set. These machines were massive, taking up an entire room or warehouse, and were very difficult to operate, let alone transport. The applications were written in machine code, which made it a very time-intensive and error-prone process. Human beings were forced to write out instructions for the machines that were structured in a way that machines could understand. This meant that human error was introduced to the equation when running any process that depended on human inputs. Errors such as typos or using the wrong function to drive an end result could make a program unusable, and identifying where the issue was in the code could be very time consuming. Computers weren't widely available or accessible, and only a small number of highly technical engineers and programmers were able to take advantage of the technology.

As the technology progressed and developed, around the 1950s and 1960s, higher-level programming languages were developed which allowed for easier use and more complex applications. It became increasingly easy to learn and build applications with simpler programming languages, allowing developers to stretch their imaginations and develop new use cases. **Object-oriented programming** began to take off, allowing engineers to only have a basic understanding of programming in order to build applications.

One of these new applications was the development of a relational database management system, a way to consistently and reliably store structured data. Languages such as FORTRAN and COBOL began to gain traction and popularity as applications began to take on use cases for database management systems. While this still typically required a monolithic approach to software development where the entire application was treated as a continuous code base, computers began to become viable for all kinds of new applications.

The 1970s and 1980s saw the rise of the personal computer as computing technology began to be compact enough to be portable yet powerful enough to run applications through a **graphical user interface** (**GUI**). The GUI made computers much more usable, even for folks who didn't have deep knowledge of computing or programming. This is a point-and-click interface where a user uses a mouse and keyboard to interact with the computing interface. It's a much more visually focused user experience compared to the command line-driven approach.

Something worth noting is that applications were still developed with the traditional mentality of one application per server and the code development was treated like a novel. Having a single code base and managing one application per server made it easier to implement security and recovery practices. However, a monolithic code base can be very difficult to manage over time and scale. Whenever a bug was identified or a new feature needed to be added, programmers would add lines of code to the code base. Over time, with growing scale and complexity, applications could become slow and struggle to execute the tasks that they were assigned to do.

The 1990s and 2000s saw the rise of the internet and web applications. This changed the game for application development given that applications could be accessed by anyone anywhere via the internet through a web browser such as Google Chrome (although Chrome wasn't around back then). These applications needed to be more scalable and performant than ever before, particularly with the rise of certain use cases such as social media platforms and massive multiplayer online games. To help with these challenges, there was also a rise in programming languages and tools, as advanced web applications needed the ability to address a wide range of needs, clients, and use cases.

Across the 2000s and 2010s, mobile phones became very advanced and eventually would become pocket-sized supercomputers. Developers had a new medium to reach users and the usage habits began to shift heavily online. Between having to develop mobile-optimized applications that could be planetary at scale while still adhering to security and compliance requirements, organizations had many challenging obstacles to overcome. Users were also spending a lot more time on the internet, with smartphones able to be continuously connected to it, creating new opportunities for engagement and monetization.

In order to deal with the growth of the internet and the expectations users had when engaging with web and mobile applications, the monolithic approach to application development became less practical. As previously mentioned, a monolithic application is an application where the code base is one continuous code base like a novel. If you try to make changes to certain parts of an application, for example, it could impact other parts of the code and have a negative impact on the application as a whole. Many organizations began to run into issues as if they were playing bug whack-a-mole—every time an issue was fixed, another issue popped up. As such, a new way to develop applications, manage code, and stimulate developer productivity was required. At the end of the day, an organization's ability to push code is correlated with its ability to fix bugs, create new features, and compete with its competitors.

Now that we have a general sense of how application development has evolved over the last few decades, let's dive into a case study to explore how this evolution took place at a hypothetical company, Acme Inc.

Acme Inc—development case study

Imagine you are a developer who has been tasked with developing an application. You have been asked to build a tool that can list the hotels within a specific area. The city you work for has a tourism division and they're hoping to expand awareness of the attractions to drive more demand and ultimately revenue. You set off to build a web application, which seems relatively simple, so you build a database that contains all the hotels in town and their address. From there, you build out a frontend for the application, which makes it easy to view and filter the different hotels that are available. The code is straightforward and relatively simple, so you decide to build a virtual machine to host the frontend of the application.

As time passes, the website begins to grow in popularity and the town is really appreciative of this push to drive awareness through digital means. People start asking for additional features to be added to the website. Maybe they want restaurants to be listed or to be able to visualize the hotels on top of a map. This will raise even more awareness for the town and tourism, so you decide to implement both! You stick with your development approach and add more lines of code to the original code base in order to support the new functionality.

Things continue to go well and now people are really starting to notice! One of the restaurants recommended on the site lands a Michelin star and a popstar from the town lands her first major single. Demand starts to balloon and people have more feature requests. You realize that the virtual machine (VM) you've set up won't be able to handle the load because demand for the web application grows, so you set up a second VM. You choose to go the VM route because you have some experience working with them and you should be able to get the environment running with minimal effort. In tandem, you start developing other features and growing the team. You bring in a junior developer to help out with coding as the feature requests grow. First, it's being able to see what kinds of nature excursions are around—parks, lakes, and trails. From there, people start requesting the ability to submit reviews, both to reward great local businesses and share negative feedback with other tourists.

After reviews, people ask for the ability to submit five-star ratings, book hotels and excursions directly through the site, and engage with local tourism experts. You and your engineer add more and more lines of code to the application to handle all of the features that are being requested. You add line after line of code and things start to go badly.

First, the application goes down after a recent code push and you can't quite figure out why. You manage to get the application live but certain components aren't working properly. Your simple web application has grown from a couple hundred lines of code to tens of thousands. Not only that, all of these lines of code are interconnected and you can't quite make out where the dependencies are and what will happen when you push new versions to production.

The more issues you have, the more lines of code you add to the application in order to solve the issue, but for every issue you solve, it seems like two bugs are found. To add even more stress to the situation, the infrastructure running the code seems to be struggling and you need bigger virtual machines. Unfortunately, the city cannot afford to upgrade the hardware within this budget cycle due to cuts related to unforeseen circumstances.

You end up in a situation where you have a big, monolithic application, meaning that the entire code base is interconnected. Given the challenges, you are stuck with a semi-functional application that isn't very reliable and prone to performance issues, with no line of sight for how this can be wholly addressed.

After fighting fires for a couple of years, you decide to explore if there are any alternatives that can both solve the infrastructure problem as well as the coding problem. You hear about new concepts of application development called **developer operations (DevOps)**, **site reliability engineering (SRE)**, containerization, and microservice-based architectures.

Now that you understand some of the challenges that development teams face, let's dive deeper into cloud-native application development and its business value.

The benefits of cloud-native application development

A **cloud-native application** is an application that is designed to take full advantage of the unique capabilities of cloud environments to maximize their agility, scalability, and resiliency. They are built with a microservices architecture in mind, benefiting from the innovation related to containerization, automation, and continuous delivery. This means taking a step back from monolithic applications, where the entire code base is one continuous, interweaving narrative, and breaking it down into more manageable components. These smaller services or microservices are blocks of code that are independent of each other and can be developed, deployed, and scaled, making the application much more flexible and scalable.

In order to understand the benefits of cloud-native development, we first need to understand what it means and the practices involved in its adoption. With applications requiring the ability to scale globally and having complex components and stringent performance requirements, a new way to build applications was required. In addition, development teams were under a lot of pressure to continuously push out new features. This meant that a new approach to development that helped teams significantly improve the speed of releases, cutting down time for launches from quarters to months to weeks or even days.

Enter the philosophy of Agile, developer productivity, and site reliability engineering. The change toward Agile was better suited to building applications in a chaotic world. Traditionally, applications had been approached in the same way as one might approach building a boat. You have a specific target architecture and you fulfill that target architecture to the exact communicated specifications. However, with the evolving needs of software users and competitive pressures, development teams found themselves having to continuously integrate and improve their products. Organizations began to think through how to maximize developer productivity while also pushing high-quality, performant code. It was identified that part of the challenge was that applications were being built like a monolith. All of the code was interwoven, and to change anything, lines of code were added to the code base. Over time, this created large applications that struggled to keep up with usage and performance requirements.

A different approach was developed where instead of treating an entire application as a whole, they would think about an application as a sum of parts that are not interconnected but actually independent of each other. This meant that one large code base could be built with a modular design resembling a Lego tower rather than a skyscraper, where there are lots of small bits of code dedicated to specific functions.

These smaller components of code can be called **services** or **microservices**. These snippets of code can be packaged in containers that are independent of each other and can run at scale much easier than monolithic code. For example, whenever you log into a website, the first service you use is the authentication service. After you log in, you check the weather and the news feed. Within a cloud-native application, you can refresh just the weather page or just the news feed without having to refresh the entire platform. This makes applications more cost-effective and scalable given that different components can scale up and down based on need. Containers also paired well with Kubernetes, allowing applications to scale horizontally based on traffic, which improved the resilience and reliability of applications. Kubernetes also helps minimize downtime and build fault tolerance into their systems. Whenever Kubernetes sees a node and associated pods fail, it can quickly spin up a new node and launch the relevant services.

These advances in building applications and hosting them led to technology teams becoming more cooperative. They began to build cross-discipline teams in order to minimize toil and maximize productivity. When spinning up a new project and assigning a team to work on it for a sprint, the team would be composed of folks from development, quality assurance, operations, and security, ensuring that teams can build and iterate quickly. Historically those teams had been relatively isolated and collaboration was a blocker to pushing new code and features.

This allowed for folks who specialize in development to focus on building code versus progressing it through its lifecycle. Similarly, by creating a focus on operational excellence, DevOps teams work proactively with other sister teams, such as security teams, to ensure that the code being developed and the production environment are designed and built with the appropriate considerations. They also implemented practices around **continuous integration and delivery (CI/CD)** pipelines, driving more automation into the application development process, which reduces the probability of human error impacting launch cycles.

To summarize, let's go ahead and review some of the advantages of cloud-native and agile application development:

- **Faster time to market**: Through the adoption of DevOps and cloud-native application development practices, organizations are able to realize meaningful efficiencies relative to the traditional approach of monolithic application development. With a focus on specialization, automation, testing, and compact, manageable code, organizations are able to push more code—at a higher quality—faster than other organizations. This can lead to a meaningful competitive advantage, as competitors will struggle to push as much code at the same level of quality without adopting similar practices.

- **Increased reliability**: Given the increase in operational rigor and automation that comes with SRE, DevOps, and cloud-native development and the underlying technologies, such as containerization or function-based computing, systems can be designed to be much more fault tolerant and reliable relative to monolithic applications. For example, if the hardware running a monolithic application goes down, so does the application. By contrast, with containers and Kubernetes, a pod of services that runs an application can quickly—and even in an automated fashion—be migrated to a new node on the cluster with little to no downtime.

- **Scalability**: Similar to reliability, one of the implications of cloud-native application development is also scalability. Where monolithic applications can only be scaled vertically, by adding more cores or memory to an existing machine, cloud-native applications are designed to scale both horizontally and vertically. This means they can allocate more machines to address a need versus trying to maximize the size of one machine. They are typically made up of many small bits of code that, when paired with Kubernetes, for example, can scale dynamically based on load or traffic. This means that cloud-native applications can scale up when there is demand for them and scale back down when there is less demand. This makes them both more scalable and cost effective, making this approach great for building externally facing applications, which expect large fluctuations in user traffic such as in gaming or e-commerce.

- **Agile culture**: The shift to an Agile culture pairs well with the shift to cloud-native development. Agile focuses on building smaller, leaner teams that can move quickly, fail fast, and iterate. This approach to application development allows for more flexibility and creativity, and teams can quickly test out new versions of an application through practices such as canary deployments and traffic splitting. This greatly increases the speed of innovation and stimulates productivity.

With a better understanding of cloud-native development, its evolution from monolithic development, and the business drivers for why an organization would adopt it, let's dive into the solutions available for hosting applications on Google Cloud and explore when they make sense.

Google Cloud solutions for hosting applications

Regardless of how mature a technology team is, they'll be able to find great hosting options for their applications on Google Cloud. Services have been launched to meet customers where they are while also enabling them to take advantage of the latest advancements in technology and cloud operations best practices. If you just need to host one virtual server or need to deploy thousands of VMs, **Google Cloud Compute Engine** is a great option. If you are an early-stage fintech start-up looking to deploy your first Kubernetes cluster, Google Cloud has **Kubernetes Engine**. Assuming you are a gaming company that wants to leverage serverless as much as possible, **Cloud Run** and **App Engine** are great options.

Let's start by exploring the traditional VM hosting options along with the relevant use cases.

Google Compute Engine (GCE)

Let's explore GCE:

- **Description**: This is Google's first-party virtualization service that allows customers to spin up virtual machines along with an ecosystem of tools to support different functionality.

- **Use case**: It is for traditional, virtual machine-based hosting. The customer will own much of the stack starting at the operating system level, selecting the appropriate OS and associated packages to run their application.

Google Cloud VMware Engine (GCVE)

Let's explore GCVE:

- **Description**: This is VMware hosting service for Google Cloud, which enables customers to make use of existing investments by allowing them to use the same toolsets and engineers to migrate and host VMware-based virtualized applications
- **Use case**: It is for migrating and hosting VMware-based virtualized workloads on Google Cloud

Sole-tenant nodes

Let's explore **sole-tenant nodes**:

- **Description**: Sole-tenant nodes are physical Compute Engine servers that are wholly dedicated to one specific customer. This provides hardware isolation, allowing customers to meet requirements around security and compliance, which require physical isolation. It can also help with meet licensing requirements in **bring your own license** (**BYOL**) scenarios that require the license to be tied to dedicated, physical hardware.
- **Use case**: It is for Windows workloads with licensing requirements, healthcare or finance workloads with security and compliance requirements, and workloads with high IOPS but low latency requirements.

Having covered the main variations of virtualization and traditional hosting, let's explore what's available for containerized workloads and serverless hosting:

Kubernetes Engine (GKE)

Let's explore GKE:

- **Description**: This is a managed Kubernetes service for running containers securely at a global scale. Google's capabilities include options such as serverless Kubernetes through autopilot, which offers a hands-off experience for running Kubernetes. It's also able to handle four-way autoscaling, allowing users to launch clusters globally with up to 15,000 nodes.
- **Use case**: It is for hosting containers on Google Cloud and running a managed Kubernetes environment. It's able to handle both stateful and stateless workloads.

Cloud Run

Let's explore Cloud Run:

- **Description**: This is a fully managed and serverless platform for hosting stateless containerized applications, services, microservices, and functions

- **Use case**: It is for hosting stateless, containerized workloads

Artifact Registry

Let's explore Artifact Registry:

- **Description**: This is the next generation of container registry, essentially allowing for the storage, management, and security for build artifacts. This includes container images and language packages.
- **Use case**: It is an artifact repository for images, CI/CD tooling, and automated pipelines.

Cloud Build

Let's explore Cloud Build:

- **Description**: This is a serverless CI/CD platform allowing customers to automate deployments at scale while retaining provenance and attestation, ensuring fast build times and prevention of tampering
- **Use case**: It is for building CI/CD or automated build pipelines in Google Cloud

App Engine

Let us explore App Engine:

- **Description**: This is a fully managed, serverless application hosting environment with advanced capabilities, such as versioning and traffic splitting
- **Use case**: It is for hosting applications with zero server management and configuration deployments

Cloud Functions

Let's explore Cloud Functions:

- **Description**: This is a Function-as-a-Service product that allows customers to run code without a server or a container. It's scalable and can scale down to 0, empowering customers to design systems that are very cost effective while still being able to handle scale.
- **Use case**: It is for event-driven or function-based computing.

Having covered the main hosting options for Google Cloud customers, let's do a quick review before we prepare to launch into the next chapter.

Summary

There are many options for customers when deciding how to host an application. If it's an existing application, considerations such as the application architecture (monolithic or microservice) or licensing restrictions will impact the decision. Ultimately, there is no *right* way to host an application without the additional context of how the code base was developed, its architecture, and the associated client requirements.

If you have an application that has operating system or database licensing requirements, you will likely opt for a sole-tenant node. Assuming you are a fresh start-up building with open source technologies in the regulated industries space building containerized applications, you'll likely end up working with Google Kubernetes Engine.

As you think through the exam questions, make sure to read the questions carefully to ensure you pick up on the keywords that are being used to designate where a workload should land. Start by thinking through whether the workload requires a virtual machine or container—is it monolithic or microservice-based? These answers will narrow down the choices of valid hosting environments and help you be successful in the exam.

9

The Value of APIs

Now that we've established a foundational understanding of application and infrastructure modernization, it's time to explore how organizations stitch different systems together to deliver a specific workflow. Often, organizations will need to integrate systems internally as well as externally to process a transaction.

This chapter covers the following topics:

- An introduction to APIs
- The value of APIs
- Full life cycle API management with Google Cloud

An introduction to APIs

Establishing connections between systems can be very challenging, depending on the use case and performance requirements. Systems need to have a way to interact with each other and programmatically retrieve information or take action. This is particularly critical when you're trying to build automation into data or DevOps pipelines where systems need to have secure communication methods and actions taken can have a meaningful impact on production environments.

Historically, integrations were custom and needed a lot of effort to be maintained. Whenever the source or destination software had an update, whether it was bug fixes or new feature sets, it would typically require a review of the integration given that the changes may have broken it. Entire technology companies began to surface and be built around system integration from both software and service perspectives. Fivetran and Airbyte are great examples of organizations that built their core value around integrating systems and data. Airbyte supports 350+ connectors (`https://airbyte.com/connectors`), including Google Cloud's Big Query and Google Ads. Indeed, system integration continues to be a prominent topic among executives and engineers alike.

In particular, data silos are perpetuated due to a lack of system integration and interoperability. This causes teams and, by extension, organizations to make decisions based on limited data, and often bad decisions end up being made because the data that's used for those decisions was questionable at best and at worst, erroneous.

The modern API as we think of it is a **web API**. It's important to note that there are also REST APIs, although folks may use the terms REST and web API interchangeably. While web APIs allow you to interact with web servers via an HTTP request, a web communication protocol for computers, REST APIs let interact with any kind of server over HTTP.

Web APIs can trace their origin to the early 2000s when online commerce began to establish itself. For e-commerce to be possible, multiple systems needed to interact with each other in an automated manner to ensure the transaction was processed quickly and correctly.

The frontend of an e-commerce site needed to load quickly, providing featured products and campaigns. When searching the product inventory, the frontend would call the inventory system to visualize specific products, their information, and whether there was stock for that product. Once the customer was ready to check out, logistics and payment systems needed to be activated to ensure the delivery was to the correct address and that the payment method was valid.

The need for fully automated workflows, particularly on the web, drove the growth and adoption of a standardized framework for system interoperability. Thus, the web API was born. Nowadays, there are many other industries and use cases where real-time system integration and data synchronization add value. Before diving into some use cases by industry, let's dig into what exactly APIs are and how they function.

When building systems that need to interact with other systems, whether internal or external, there needs to be a way to establish communication between them for them to exchange information or trigger an action. An API is a standardized method of executing this transaction between systems, where one system reaches out to the other for a specific set of information or action and the other responds accordingly, for example with a message that contains the requested information.

An **API endpoint** is the location from which the request is received and action is taken. This is typically a URL endpoint that systems can call and get a response from. The source system makes a call to the API endpoint in the form of a request message and the API endpoint provides an appropriate response, either a message containing the results of the action or the requested data.

The most common communication protocol implementations of APIs are **Hypertext Transfer Protocol (HTTP)**, **JavaScript Object Notation (JSON)**, and **Extensible Markup Language (XML)**. By having API responses built with a specific structure, systems that receive those responses can then process the request in an automated manner that won't require human revision or engagement to ensure the accuracy of the workflow. Automated workflows free up human brain power and time to focus on other activities that may be more suited to humans.

Now that we have a foundational understanding of APIs and why organizations began using them, let's explore the specific value that they can provide to both traditional and modern organizations.

The value of APIs

As you can imagine from the first section of this chapter, APIs can apply to any company or industry that needs to provide data to its customers or partners. Whether it's an e-commerce company surfacing real-time inventory data, an airline providing real-time visibility into seat availability for its flights, or an academic institution that is making data available to researchers worldwide – APIs can be a valuable component of building for scale and automation.

The human approach to retrieving data can be very time-consuming and prone to human error. For example, let's say the sales team would like to get a sense of the revenue being driven by a product catalog for the fiscal year. Historically, this request would have to be submitted to a business analyst or operations team member who would then have to figure out how to collect all of the data. The sales team may need information about historical spending and growth month over month or year over year, broken down by geography and industry.

Assuming an organization breaks down a product portfolio into separate product teams and each product team only has visibility into their data – with no centralized data repository nor any way to programmatically build a report on top of shared data – the person responsible would likely have to spend days, if not weeks, understanding who has access to what data and who can pull reports on that data, ensuring that the reports are pulled with the right parameters and then marry the reports into a single, unified report.

What if this workflow needed to be repeated quarterly, monthly, or even weekly? Business operations folks would have to spend hours on a repetitive task just to generate reports that are prone to human errors such as pulling stale data, incorrect data, or even falsified data.

In a world where the business has API interfaces for all of its systems and aggregates this information in an automated manner regularly within a data warehouse where sales teams and their supporting cast can self-serve data, the entirety of the preceding workflow is eliminated through automation. Data is pulled regularly from all of the source systems and landed in a centralized repository that essentially becomes a data mart for the company. Precautions will likely need to be taken, such as restricting the views of different teams depending on their roles, to not unnecessarily expose sensitive data, but the business becomes much more agile. Rather than focusing time and effort on triaging, collecting, and consolidating data, the focus is on taking action based on the data and designing GTM strategies enabled by the data.

Let's explore some of the benefits of leveraging APIs for traditional companies.

Creating new products, services, and monetization streams

By layering APIs on top of existing applications and systems, organizations can derive new value from existing investments. Whether that's launching a new service that provides real-time information where historically it was batched data or new integrations, many new possibilities open up on the horizon.

Real-time data is very powerful, depending on the industry. For example, in e-commerce, if you begin using real-time weather data to influence marketing campaigns, you can produce highly targeted and localized recommendations. This might mean launching campaigns for raincoats, umbrellas, and boots whenever a storm is about to roll into a set of states. For an airline, real-time weather patterns will impact air traffic routes and flight times, allowing them to dynamically optimize routes and times to minimize customer impact from predicted weather events.

For traditional organizations, this might mean even opening up access to its proprietary data to partners and the government. Assuming you're a logistics organization, you may want to provide real-time visibility for deliveries, whether the end client is a consumer or a government agency, and even charge extra for it, depending on the circumstances.

Improving the client experience

Traditional organizations tend to pass on the burden of their technical debt to the customer experience. Systems tend to be slower, less responsive, and often less secure. Providing an API interface through which folks can interact with their systems and data allows for a layer of abstraction that can obscure some of the challenges associated with legacy systems. You can essentially strip services out of a monolithic application via APIs and build additional tools, systems, and applications on top of it.

This can mean that you build an improved, modern customer experience on top of a legacy system. You make the legacy system integrate and take action based on instructions from other systems built on top of it that provide a positive client experience.

An example would be instead of having a human internally pull reports for clients based on written/email parameters, you can provide clients and their teams with an API interface through which they can pull reports themselves – with a set of permissions and restrictions to ensure that they only have visibility into the appropriate data.

Now that we've explored some of the benefits for traditional companies to leverage APIs, let's go ahead and explore the benefits for modern or digital native companies as well.

Quick and easy interoperability between cloud systems

Cloud-native or digital-native companies, within the world of Google Cloud, are organizations that were born in the cloud or have wholeheartedly embraced the cloud-native way of working. This means building systems in the cloud with a focus on being able to quickly and easily integrate with other systems. You might expose a model or service via API that makes it very easy to use within your infrastructure or even as a product to be consumed externally.

These organizations can have numerous integrations with third parties as part of the value that they provide to their clients. If someone is building a data company, for example, where they provide a platform that aggregates third-party and public datasets along with a set of tooling to help folks derive value from these data, they might require hundreds of integrations.

By having a standard method and set of protocols through which to integrate with countless external systems, cloud-native organizations can quickly and easily interact with all of these external systems in an automated manner to minimize the overhead cost of having a human-centric approach to their business.

Building for scale and resiliency

APIs not only make it easy for applications to interact with each other, by defining a standardized communication method, but they can also be highly scalable. Given that traffic for different services or components of an application tends to vary based on time of day and usage patterns, APIs allow you to grow the underlying infrastructure to handle the request traffic for specific components of a system. For example, whenever users log in for their workday, the first thing they do is authenticate. From there, they may need to access their emails to review what business communications they have received. Communication is business critical to ensure that an organization executes its functions efficiently and effectively. However, traffic patterns for folks accessing, reviewing, and sending emails may fluctuate wildly throughout the day.

By putting the mail service behind an API, infrastructure teams can ensure that the infrastructure can scale up based on the requests and then scale back down when it's no longer needed. Traffic can be distributed to several instances and assuming the number of instances isn't appropriate, it can automatically grow or reduce the instance pool to handle the traffic accordingly in a cost-effective manner.

API requests can also fail gracefully, helping with system resiliency. This means that they can be designed to automatically retry requests that fail, which helps prevent outages and system issues that can arise from glitches or bugs.

Now that we understand the value of APIs, let's explore Google Cloud's enterprise-grade solution for API management, Apigee.

Full life cycle API management with Google Cloud

Google Cloud has a product named Apigee that is specifically designed for full life cycle API management. It allows for the establishment of an API proxy layer that sits between a client's backend infrastructure and access to its services and data. Apigee is particularly powerful because beyond providing an API endpoint, it also has a wide range of tools and capabilities that are required when building enterprise-grade APIs.

With APIs being the fabric through which systems interact, both internally and externally, there are many important considerations when making them accessible. For example, clients can benefit from out-of-the-box policies in Apigee that help implement the appropriate controls around security, traffic, data access, extensions, and beyond. Apigee also allows for customization through things such as custom code, conditions, rate limiting, and many other actions that are relevant for mature APIs and the teams that manage them.

Some of the key benefits of Apigee are as follows:

- Discoverability and community
- Insights
- Reliability

Let's look at them in detail.

Discoverability and community

Once an API is production-ready and has been published, the next step is generating demand for the API. With Apigee comes access to the Apigee producer portal, where other developers can learn about your API and its documentation, start building applications with it, and register as a developer, allowing them to receive updates regarding launches and changes to the API.

Insights

APIs also need to be managed and monitored after launch. Apigee provides toolsets to help with advanced security capabilities, infrastructure monitoring, and usage insights. By providing security reports and abuse detection, developers can have visibility into security threats such as bots impacting an API, along with traffic analysis, which can be used to indicate malicious activity.

You can even take security actions based on triggers from the abuse detection service. For example, if a specific IP or set of IPs has been recognized to have consistent, malicious traffic patterns, you can implement a security action to block traffic or requests from those malicious IPs.

Reliability

By being hosted on Google Cloud, Apigee benefits from Google's underlying infrastructure and networking to be highly available and reliable. In addition, by decoupling client API requests from the backend infrastructure, changes can be made to the backend without any interruption to clients who may be consuming the API. Also, by programmatically implementing infrastructure and security controls, the producer of the API can ensure that policies are applied consistently and are therefore compliant with any client demands or relevant government legislation.

Apigee is well regarded as one of the most mature API full life cycle management solutions, as highlighted by its recognition as a leader in Gartner's 2022 analysis (`https://cloud.google.com/blog/products/api-management/apigee-is-a-leader-in-the-gartner-mq-for-api-management`).

Summary

APIs have become a critical piece of building and integrating cloud systems. Not only do they help with automating processes and workflows, they also help create new opportunities for organizations, regardless of whether they're traditional or cloud-native. Through the adoption of a mature, enterprise-ready API full life cycle management solution such as Apigee, organizations can build and manage complex integrations for both customers and partners while ensuring the security, reliability, and scalability of their solutions.

Next, we'll dive into Google Cloud's approach to security and an exploration of the first-party solutions that are available to customers who want to improve their security posture.

Part 4: Understanding Google Cloud Security and Operations

The fourth part of this book will focus on Google's approach to security and IT operation best practices. The security portion will highlight how Google differentiates itself when it comes to security, given its focus on securing customers beyond the bounds of the shared responsibility model. We'll also discuss key concepts and best practices to manage infrastructure in cloud environments, such as service availability, DevOps, and SRE.

This part has the following chapters:

- *Chapter 10, Google Cloud's Approach to Security*
- *Chapter 11, IT Operations in the Cloud*
- *Chapter 12, Resource Monitoring and Application Performance Management on Google Cloud*

10

Google Cloud's Approach to Security

This chapter will help readers understand some of the foundational principles of security in the cloud space, particularly Google Cloud. We'll go over things such as the **shared responsibility model**, understand the differences between Google's approach to security relative to other providers, and dig into the threats to privacy. Lastly, we'll explore how to properly control and manage cloud resources.

After completing this chapter, you will be able to do the following:

- Understand the core concepts of securing a cloud environment and data privacy
- Describe the security benefits of using Google Cloud
- Identify today's top cybersecurity challenges and threats to data privacy
- Describe important controls for managing and securing cloud resources

The chapter covers the following topics:

- Security fundamentals
- Overview of the shared responsibility model
- The benefits and differentiators of Google Cloud
- Controlling and managing cloud resources

Security fundamentals

Security is a topic that can feel overwhelming, particularly as you start to dig deeper into the tech stack. In this chapter, we'll explore the most important topics relating to the certification exam. You can think of this as a simplified introduction, touching on different attack vectors, approaches to compromising systems, and the associated defense strategies.

At a very high level, there are two types of attacks: **social engineering** and **technical engineering**. Social engineering refers to the exploitation of humans in order to obtain information that will help compromise a system or obtain sensitive information. This is a very common attack vector and is often connected to phishing. **Phishing** is when an attacker sends malicious emails, for example, to a set of legitimate users in the hopes that they will be compromised. This can be a fake landing page asking them to sign into a website, which then captures their login credentials for accessing systems.

Social engineering can take many forms, including phone calls claiming to be an executive and using that to manipulate employees. Even showing up to an office location with fake or stolen equipment is a common method of testing an organization's security. Whether it's done through email, phone calls, or in person, social engineering strives to manipulate human beings to reach a specific outcome for an attacker.

Beyond social engineering, malicious actors may also try to penetrate systems by exploiting misconfigurations, known vulnerabilities, or zero-day vulnerabilities, which are new vulnerabilities. This may mean scanning devices on a network to see if any of them are exposed to the internet and contain useful information. It may mean brute-forcing a password, assuming there aren't proper advanced controls, such as password lock-out or multi-factor authentication.

Ultimately, competent attackers will weave together both approaches to drive a specific outcome. Cyberattacks tend to follow a relatively consistent pattern: recon, weaponization, delivery, exploitation, back door installation, call home, and take action on the objective.

Reconnaissance refers to the gathering of information to facilitate the exploitation. This will include gathering public information online, potentially trying to get employees to divulge sensitive information, and scanning the target network for a compromisable system. Once you have a general sense of the target environment, the attacker may craft or procure software that will be used to carry out the attack. A nation state might decide to build a new, specific, and unique set of software and tools to maximize impact and minimize traceability. Meanwhile, an average malicious actor might procure malicious software from the darknet or even use open source tooling, such as what's built into Kali Linux, a Linux distribution built for security researchers and practitioners.

Once the attack has been planned out, the attacker then needs to penetrate the system somehow. This may mean compromising an employee's credentials or exploiting an issue with how the system was configured or a vulnerability in the code. Once a network has been penetrated, the payload is installed on a machine—whether it's a desktop or a server—and calls back to the command and control center for instructions. Depending on the circumstances, the command and control center may instruct the software to hibernate, capture data, or even exfiltrate data. Assuming the machine that was penetrated was not the ultimate target, the payload could be a worm, which compromises additional machines on the network.

Assuming the target is the exfiltration of intellectual property or the encryption of sensitive data, the attack is complete once the information has been stolen or the ransom is paid. With more advanced attackers, long-term espionage in itself may be the goal and so the game becomes how to steal as much information without triggering the defense of the defender.

Now that we understand how attackers think and how their attacks are carried out, let's explore how defenders respond to these attacks.

A big part of the challenge of being a defender is that you have to be consistently excellent at your job. You must ensure that all of your systems are secure, running up-to-date operating systems with the latest patches and accompanying visibility tooling such as antivirus scanning. Tooling and policies that ensure compliance with security guidance are critical to maintaining a secure environment.

Preventative security is a great approach to ensuring you are catching things before they enter your network. This involves the implementation of tools that are able to assess the risk of a file or link before a user engages with it. This kind of network-level scanning and blocking can be implemented to inspect email and web traffic, ensuring things such as malicious links and attachments are never surfaced to users. When in doubt, advanced systems can even quarantine high-risk files and detonate them in a sandbox in order to verify if there is any malicious code.

In addition to ensuring proper visibility and patching practices, security teams also need to have clear and concise procedures for how to handle identity and access management. The principle of least privilege is the idea that a user should only be able to access data and systems that are required to do the job. There is no reason why a salesperson, for example, should be able to access a company's code base. Inversely, a software developer should have neither visibility nor access to sensitive client information unless it's expressly required for their job. Defining and managing permissions for both users and services is a critical function of security teams, as this will minimize the attack surface assuming someone does get phished. Tools and technologies can help. For example, **multi-factor authentication** (MFA) forces an employee to prove through multiple mechanisms that they are indeed the legitimate user.

Factors of authentication are essentially ways through which you can prove you are who you say you are. There are three buckets of factors: *something you know*, *something you have*, and *something you are*. Something you know would be a username and password combination. Something you have would be a USB key or some other physical token that can validate your identity. Another example of something you have would be a driver's license or the key to your house. Something you are refers to a biological indicator such as a fingerprint or retina scan.

In order to protect an organization from social engineering attacks, it takes both human and technical safeguards. From a human perspective, policies and training should be implemented to ensure employees are skeptical and always validate access rights before divulging any sensitive information. This includes phishing simulations, where employees are sent fake phishing emails to gauge how gullible and aware they are. Making sure to always verify someone's identity, whether over the phone or in person, is also critical in ensuring that social engineers don't drive their target outcome.

Assuming an attacker is able to penetrate your defenses, you also need tools that will provide visibility into your infrastructure and detect potential threats. This may mean anomalous activity, such as a server making a call to the external command and control center or a user logging in and exfiltrating data at 3 a.m. on a Saturday. Advanced organizations with more mature security postures may even have tooling that prevents data exfiltration. An example of this is disabling USB drive connectivity, printer connectivity, or the ability to block sending files and attachments to a personal email account.

As you can imagine, securing a large technology estate can become extremely difficult, costly, and time consuming. Between ensuring the physical security of the data centers, that software is up to date, and that all of your employees are responsible, it can be very overwhelming.

Understanding challenges and threats to data

Beyond software and hardware security, customers and their technology teams must also account for compliance legislation, copyright considerations, and customer sensitivity when making decisions related to how they use and manage their data. Some of the most common compliance requirements in the United States are **Personal Identifiable Information (PII)**, **Payment Card Industry Data Security Standard (PCI-DSS)**, **Personal Health Information (PHI)**, **Health Insurance Portability and Accountability Act (HIPAA)**, **Children's Online Privacy Protect Act (COPPA)**, and **Federal Risk and Authorization Management Program (FedRAMP)**. Organizations that serve clients globally will also need to be cognizant of major regional and international compliance standards as well, such as the **General Data Protection Regulation (GDPR)** in the European Union and the **International Organization for Standardization (ISO)** requirements for data center compliance.

What these standards have in common is that they're designed to define a set of expectations for how sensitive data should be stored, processed, made available, and monetized. In order to maintain compliance with some or all of these standards, organizations will need to put in place personnel, policies, technologies, and practices to ensure consistent compliance. This may mean hosting data in specific regions and only processing it in a certain way based on data localization and processing legislation.

An organization may implement data access and security controls even if they don't necessarily have compliance-driven justification to do so. In order to protect their intellectual property and copyrighted content, companies need to ensure that they have the appropriate security posture to protect their data. Assuming they have their clients using their tools with proprietary data, customer trust and retention are also drivers in adopting advanced security practices.

Over the last couple of decades, the rise of companies such as Google, Facebook, Amazon, and others has led to the rise of big data and the data economy. Data creates a lot of opportunity for organizations given that they can use data to make better decisions and create value for their clients. However, by digitizing processes and data, the threat landscape for technology also evolves. In order to build cloud-native, data-centric organizations, you also need to adopt cloud-native security practices.

Organizations need to be aware of all the threats and challenges when handling data in order to build a strong security foundation and address the needs of their ecosystem. Threats include nation states that may be trying to steal their intellectual property or more generally cause chaos through ransomware or the interruption of service.

Their competitors may even engage in espionage in order to understand competitive differentiation, deal structures, and go-to-market strategies. This may surface as social engineering, or they may even hire agents to conduct cyber espionage operations. This is commonly referred to as an **insider threat**. Being aware of the threat insiders pose is critical given that data may be exposed with or without malicious intent. For example, an employee may try to get a head start on a project by sharing sensitive materials with an external partner that's not under a **non-disclosure agreement** (**NDA**). Depending on the sensitivity of the data, having the ability to document the security incident, control the damage, and educate employees to avoid similar issues in the future is very important.

Insiders can also become a threat due to personal issues such as being impacted by internal decisions that have negative consequences on a project or promotion decision. Someone who has had their project terminated by leadership may decide that they want to continue working on the project–on their own time or at a competitor to their current employer–and therefore try to exfiltrate their work. This may be as simple as emailing documents or uploading them to a personal email or storage service.

Whether a threat is external or internal, organizations need to ensure they have the appropriate systems, controls, and practices in place to identify security risks, stop them before they do damage, and contain the damage if an operation does have some level of success.

Beyond malicious or accidental leaks, a company may have to implement privacy and security practices to build client trust and differentiate itself from its competitors. Over the years, Google has positioned many products, with security being one of the core differentiators. Whether we're talking about the Chrome browser, Chrome Operating system, or Google Cloud, Google made the decision to take an approach to security where everything is built to be secure by default. This stands in contrast to other vendors who may not prioritize security and experience much higher rates of 0-day vulnerabilities in the wild and compromises that lead to significant negative impacts on their clients.

These threats can be identified and thwarted at the network level, the endpoint level, or the application level. Organizations with mature security practices will have deployed tools that help them control access to sensitive files and systems. They'll also have visibility into file access and system behavior and the ability to remediate issues as they arise. Their security teams will be equipped with investigative tools and automation, helping them quickly identify issues when they happen and even automate remediation. For example, if an employee accidentally exposes an internally facing database to the public internet, a visibility tool can trigger an alert to the security team. In an autonomous world, the systems may even be able to create a firewall rule that prevents database access from the public internet as a way of addressing the issue, freeing up security engineers for more complex projects and tasks.

The good news is that the same approach that is taken to make general business data valuable can also be applied to security data. Organizations use technologies to have real-time visibility into their systems and network health in order to quickly identify and remediate issues. **Security Information and Event Management** (**SIEM**) systems are used to consolidate security telemetry from different systems and help security teams triage issues.

At scale, managing all of the security or privacy requirements and ensuring an organization is compliant with the relevant regulations can be challenging and very daunting. This requires full visibility into technology systems, ensuring that everything is patched, up to date, and supported. You also need tools and systems to identify issues, whether from an error or a malicious action, in order to remediate them as quickly as possible.

As you can imagine, part of the drive to the cloud for many organizations is the fact that they can offload part of this responsibility to cloud providers. In the next part of this chapter, we'll go deeper into the shared responsibility model for the cloud and how it helps customers with their security posture.

Overview of the shared responsibility model

The shared responsibility model is a concept relating to the delineation of responsibility when someone adopts a cloud solution. Depending on the solution and its architecture, a cloud provider will take ownership of ensuring the security up to a certain level of the technology stack, beyond which the customer is responsible. It defines a set of responsibilities to be designated across portions of the stack. These responsibilities include the hardware, boot, hardened kernel and **inter-process communication (IPC)**, storage and encryption, network, audit logging, operating systems and logging, network security, access and authentication, operations, identity, web application security, deployment, usage, access policy, and content/data.

If an organization is running its infrastructure on premises within its own data centers, it is responsible for everything. It must procure the hardware and software, ensure it is hardened and patched, manage the storage of information and its security, and ensure that they have visibility into who is accessing what systems. In addition to setting up the foundational infrastructure for its application, it also needs to ensure that everything is secure and compliant in terms of authentication, identity, application vulnerabilities, access control, and data.

In order to manage all of this at scale, an organization essentially needs to become an expert in building and running data centers. While large, traditional companies may not think much of this investment in time, expertise, and materials, younger organizations or those that are growing quickly cannot afford those same investments. For a startup to build out a data center, it could cost hundreds of thousands of dollars and take years, and it would need to hire physical and cybersecurity specialists to manage its infrastructure. This essentially becomes a blocker for growth given the physical constraints around procuring land and building a data center.

The first wave of the cloud was the **software-as-a-service (SaaS)** revolution. Rather than having to procure software and install it on a local server, clients were able to procure and use software directly through the internet. This means that the SaaS provider delivers an application to their clients through a browser, and all the client needs to do to use it is configure it for their use case and upload the relevant data. Companies such as Salesforce rose as a part of this wave given that the digitization and consolidation of processes within cloud SaaS systems allowed for all new use cases such as automation and integrations. Workers were liberated from working at a desk in an office because their work could be accessible from anywhere in the world. This also led to the rise of laptops and mobile applications given that workers were an internet connection away from being productive.

The infrastructure wave of cloud computing, which kicked off around 2010, helped alleviate much of the pain around building infrastructure and spawned a new age of technology startups. Rather than having to build out infrastructure, they can leverage an existing infrastructure platform and create infrastructure through a GUI interface or an API. Startups and other technology companies were given a tool that not only helped ensure that they had a stronger security posture with fewer resources but also a flexible environment that could grow with them as they matured. When using the cloud for virtualization or as an **infrastructure-as-a-service** (**IaaS**) solution, the cloud provider takes ownership of the tech stack from the hardware up through to audit logging. This means that the physical security of the infrastructure, the boot and kernel, storage, and networking is managed by the provider. Everything above that layer, however, remains the responsibility of the client. The client essentially takes on the responsibility of managing everything in the stack above the operating systems, including network security, authentication, and web application security.

The latest evolution in cloud computing has been the rise of **platform as a service** (**PaaS**), where cloud providers deliver developer tooling within the cloud to make it easier and more secure to build and launch new applications. PaaS sits between SaaS and IaaS in the sense that the client is responsible for more than they would be if using a SaaS solution but less than if they were using an IaaS solution. Namely, when using PaaS tools, the cloud provider takes ownership of everything they would for IaaS but also the operating system layer, network security, authentication, operations, and identity management. Clients would still need to be responsible for things such as the **Open Worldwide Application Security Project** (**OWASP**) for web application security, deployment, usage, and beyond.

Although the shared security model has been the standard for the cloud industry for over a decade, customers are still experiencing security incidents. Cloud security breaches are often caused by things that can be associated with human error, such as mistakes directly related to a misconfiguration or insufficient key and identity management, as highlighted by the *Cloud Security Alliance threat report* (2022) (`https://cloudsecurityalliance.org/press-releases/2022/06/07/cloud-security-alliance-s-top-threats-to-cloud-computing-pandemic-11-report-finds-traditional-cloud-security-issues-becoming-less-concerning/`).

Google in particular is trying to stand out from the industry by raising the bar for the responsibility of cloud providers. Rather than ignoring issues that arise from the current model, Google Cloud believes in the idea of a shared fate model where the cloud providers should go out of their way to ensure that their clients are safe, even if this means stretching beyond the delineation of the shared responsibility model.

For example, by building and providing tools such as the **Security and Command Center** (**SCC**) for customers, Google Cloud helps them monitor their environment and provides fine-grained visibility into their cloud environments. This can be very helpful in helping proactively identify issues, remediate them, and even build automation into security policies. SCC can even help customers monitor and manage regulatory compliance for their Google Cloud environment.

In the next section, we'll explore Google Cloud's security posture and its differentiators at a high level before diving into specific differentiators.

The benefits and differentiators of Google Cloud

As highlighted in previous chapters, one of the biggest advantages that Google Cloud has over its competitors is the fact that Google Cloud is built on top of Google infrastructure. This means that Google Cloud customers benefit from many of the technological advances and best practices developed by Google. This includes leveraging a global, proprietary network where all data is encrypted at rest and in transit by default. In addition, Google security teams are engaged in ensuring that the underlying network and data center infrastructure is hardened enough to fight off even the most advanced threats. With Google having 10+ applications with over 500 million users and several with over 1 billion users, their security teams are exposed to threats from all over the world on a daily basis. They then take the knowledge from these attacks, such as malware signatures, and build solutions and defenses, equipping themselves with some of the most advanced security capabilities in the world.

Beyond malware awareness, the Google team also takes physical security very seriously. This includes MFA on server-side infrastructure through a Google-designed Titan security chip—a hardware validation layer to prove that machines connecting to the Google network are legitimate and have the proper access rights.

Google Cloud has also acquired several entities to strengthen its overall security posture and story, as highlighted by the recent addition of Mandiant to the portfolio, a globally renowned security consulting firm. Between the extremely competent and capable Google security teams, their hardware and software security practices, and the technologies available through Google Cloud for customers, folks are equipped to build highly secure and resilient systems.

In this section, we'll explore some of the security products and services available to Google Cloud customers.

Security Command Center

SCC is a solution built into Google Cloud that provides visibility into issues such as misconfigurations and potential vulnerabilities within the environment. It allows organizations to quickly identify where there may be issues and provides a prioritization layer, equipping folks with the information they need to address security incidents based on urgency. As part of this visibility, it's also able to identify issues that are specific to certain compliance requirements.

You can almost think of SCC as lightweight **security information and event management** (**SIEM**), although it's not meant to aggregate security logs from different, external environments. At its heart, SCC is a security posture visibility and remediation tool designed specifically for Google Cloud environments and is only meant to aggregate information from one GCP organization's projects and folders.

Cloud Armor

Cloud Armor is a network security service that protects Google Cloud customers from web and Denial-of-Service (DoS) attacks. It is able to detect and mitigate attacks against load balancing services such as the Layer 7 global load balancing service. **Machine learning** (**ML**)-based mechanisms are used to understand traffic patterns for different applications and then to help detect and block DDoS attacks. It can also be used to help protect from the top 10 OWASP security risks for web applications. Lastly, Cloud Armor allows customers to implement rate limiting for their applications, allowing them to implement rules that protect their applications from large volumes of requests, which may throttle access for legitimate users.

Chronicle SIEM

The Chronicle SIEM solution is Google's approach to managing the proliferation of security logs and systems. Traditional SIEMs can be very expensive solutions and only retain information for a small window of time. By bringing Google's best-in-class search capabilities and marrying them with its big data warehousing technology, Chronicle SIEM delivers a next-generation experience where petabytes of data can be queried in seconds, allowing security analysts and researchers to quickly run investigations and take action.

In addition to sheer scale and speed, Chronicle is also valuable in investigating advanced threats given that it can retain logs for up to a year. This means that whenever a breach is identified, security teams will have a much richer data environment to understand what happened, how the attacker got into the network, and what, if anything, was exfiltrated.

Chronicle SOAR

The Chronicle **Security Orchestration, Automation, and Response** (**SOAR**) solution is a platform that allows security teams to build automation into and streamline their workflows. It provides a GUI where even folks without a development or coding background can quickly identify issues, design workflows, and automate remediation. It also leverages Google's ML capabilities to help response teams quickly identify and address issues as they arise in real time. Through the adoption of a solution that drives automated response, Chronicle SOAR users are able to reinforce their security posture by reducing response times to identify and remediate threats.

Mandiant incident response and threat awareness

Mandiant is a mature security firm that offers both technologies and services to its clients. Mandiant in particular shines in terms of its incident response team. Whenever an attacker is able to penetrate a network, the defender needs to take action in order to remove their access. This can be very difficult and stressful to do assuming an IT team doesn't have experience or policy to fall back on regarding how to respond. Mandiant incident response provides clients with an investigation team that can hunt for active threats, analyze an ongoing breach, engage in crisis management, and help the business recover from the fallout of an attack.

In addition to incident response services, Mandiant also has technologies such as its threat intelligence solution, which allows customers to have the latest information regarding threats in the wild. This allows security teams to proactively identify defenses and vulnerabilities, equipping them with the information required to operationalize threat information.

Now that we've explored some of the specific technologies and benefits of building infrastructure on Google Cloud, let's explore how to control and manage cloud resources.

Controlling and managing cloud resources

When managing cloud resources, we can roughly break things down into two buckets; **identity and access management** (**IAM**) and operations. Within the world of IAM, we'll explore how resource hierarchies and permissions function in Google Cloud. In the following chapters, we'll dig specifically into logging, monitoring, and best practices. Let's start by digging into IAM and resource hierarchies.

IAM and resource hierarchies

As highlighted in this chapter, a significant component of managing security is the ability to manage access and permissions. Within a Google Cloud environment, there is a resource hierarchy. An organization node is the root authority for an organization underneath which the rest of the resource hierarchy unfolds. Within an organization exist folders and projects. Folders are used to organize multiple projects and assign a set of permissions. Beneath folders in the hierarchy are projects, and within projects, resources are activated to deliver the cloud infrastructure and platform services.

Google Cloud Resource Manager allows customers to implement access control and organizational policies as appropriate, ensuring that only folks who need access to a project or folder have it:

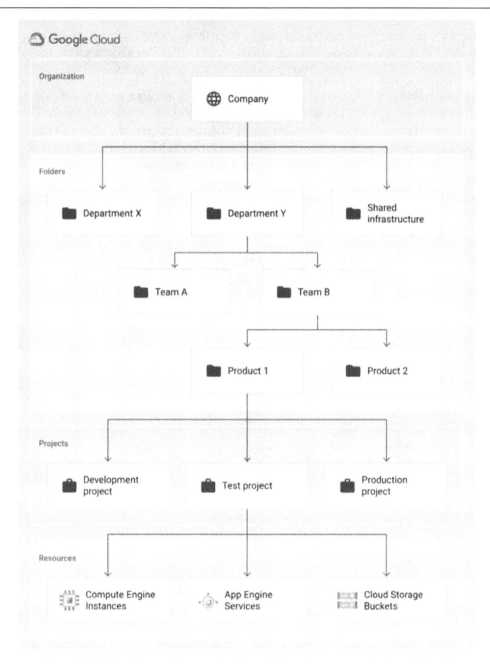

Figure 10.1 – Breakdown of an organization and hierarchy structure in Google Cloud
(source: https://cloud.google.com/resource-manager/docs/cloud-platform-resource-hierarchy)

An organization may have several folders and projects depending on how it is organized. For example, the team for a specific application can be assigned a folder, and within that folder are three additional folders that segment the development, staging, and production environments.

Cloud Identity is Google Cloud's IAM service, which allows you to assign a user specific roles and permissions associated with their function. Something it's important to keep in mind with Google Cloud is that everything has an identity—even infrastructure. For example, whenever assigning permissions to a server or application, a service account needs to be created and attached to that machine in order for the IAM policies to apply. A **service account** is essentially a user account that's generated but assigned to an application or compute instance, for example. This allows applications to make calls to APIs through their service accounts and have them authenticate, propagating the permissions assigned to the service account to the application.

When managing IAM, whether discussing users or service accounts, it's important to think about the principle of least privilege and managing privileges by groups rather than users. The **principle of least privilege** is the idea that any set of permissions assigned to a user or service account should contain only the access required for it to perform its functions. This means that someone on the marketing team should not have access to the code base or customer contracts. This also means that a machine that is granted permissions through a service account should only be mapped with the access it requires to execute its tasks. If it doesn't need access to the data warehouse to perform its tasks, it shouldn't have permission to access, read, or change information in the data warehouse. Whenever folks are new to IAM or set up policies incorrectly, they can accidentally expose their organization to risks such as leaving a database exposed to the internet or giving a machine access to systems or information that it otherwise shouldn't have. By establishing user or service roles and groups—managing permissions at this higher level of abstraction—security and operations teams can ensure that they aren't accidentally overprovisioning permissions, which can put the company at risk. The alternative is having many individuals and service accounts with different permission sets, which may or may not be relevant for their roles at a point in time. Managing permissions on an individual basis can be very time consuming and risky given that you would need to validate each individual's needs and permissions, increasing the probability of human error and an unnecessarily expansive scope of permissions.

Another principle within Google Cloud IAM is that roles and permissions are assigned top-down but cannot be forced from the bottom up. Another way to think about this is that permissions that are assigned at a higher level of abstraction, such as the Org node or a folder, will be inherited by its subfolders and projects. Therefore, if someone is assigned a project editor permission at the folder level and the folder has three projects, the person will have project editor permission for all three projects. If the permissions for project editor are assigned at the project level for one project, however, they would only have permissions for that specific project. These permissions would not roll up to the folder level or across to the other projects.

Now that we have an understanding of permissions, let's explore how they are implemented and managed in Google Cloud.

Operations

In this part of the chapter, we'll focus on how to operationalize the security concepts around IAM on Google Cloud before discussing cloud IT operations more broadly in the following chapters.

Cloud Identity is a platform that unifies identity, access, and endpoint management into one solution. This allows customers to have a central management plane for ensuring that users and infrastructure have access relevant to their roles while minimizing unnecessary exposure to risk. Customers can leverage Cloud Identity to implement **single sign-on** (**SSO**), which serves as a central authentication service. With SSO, security teams eliminate the need for users to memorize multiple passwords across different systems. This significantly reduces the risk around password management given the historic issues with unsafe password practices, such as having passwords that are too short, reusing passwords, and having to constantly reset passwords for users that are locked out. Security teams are also able to implement rigor around authentication, such as MFA, as highlighted previously in the chapter.

In addition to simplifying permissions and authentication, Cloud Identity has the added benefit of being able to manage user devices. The endpoint management capabilities include the ability to remotely wipe devices that may have been lost or stolen, deploy applications, and generate end user reports, among other capabilities. These capabilities allow you to implement security controls through technology and automation, reducing the risk and toil faced by security teams.

Google Cloud also provides tooling that helps expand visibility and control over what access Google admins have through transparency tooling and approval flows. Through the terms of service for Google Cloud, (`https://cloud.google.com/terms`), customers are contractually guaranteed the following:

> *Google will only access, use, and otherwise process Customer Data in accordance with the Cloud Data Processing Addendum and will not access, use, or process Customer Data for any other purpose. Google has implemented and will maintain technical, organizational, and physical measures to protect Customer Data, as further described in the Cloud Data Processing Addendum.*

In order to ensure customer data is protected, Google Cloud provides customers with admin access logs so that customers understand when, how, and why their data was accessed. As highlighted by the contractual language, Google will not use customer data unless expressly approved by the customer within the scope of a Data Processing Addendum. **Data Processing Addendums** are only put in place with customer execution and are typically related to participating in the development cycle of Google Cloud products. They specifically define what data can be used and for what purpose.

Customers also have the ability to implement controls regarding resource usage through resource quotas and budgets within the Google Cloud console. Resource permissions and quotas limit which and how many resources are allocated to a project. For example, before being able to access a compute engine, a user must be provisioned with the appropriate permissions to enable the API and spin up infrastructure. Enabling APIs and assigning the proper permissions are a big part of how Google Cloud ensures customers aren't unaware of their users spinning up resources and projects. Once a project and user have the associated permissions, they also need to ensure they've requested the appropriate resources. Customers and their admins can limit the resources assigned to a project and, by extension, its cost. For example, they may request a specific amount of compute and memory for a project but not allow the project to go beyond a threshold. This may surface to users as a limit of 100 cores or 2 TB of RAM for a project. Google Cloud is built to have services locked down by default, meaning that to access any service or API, a customer admin must specifically allow access through permissions and assign a quota to a user or project. This adds both technical and financial security to GCP deployments by cutting down on shadow IT and ensuring that administrators are assigning access, permissions, and associated quotas.

Customers are also able to establish a relative level of financial governance through billing alerts. Billing alerts allow you to define cost milestones and trigger alerts so that infrastructure teams are aware of projects that may be consuming ahead of schedule. This could be an early warning that a system has an issue that needs to be investigated or a project is increasing in scope and will likely go over the budget.

Summary

Ensuring that Google Cloud customers have a strong security posture, built with security best practices in mind, gives Google a very strong position in the market. Customers are able to confidently deploy sensitive infrastructure and data in the environment while also ensuring they remain compliant with any legal or customer requirements.

A strong security foundation is critical in driving innovation, especially in the age of big data and AI where issues such as copyright infringement, strict compliance needs, and cost need to be balanced with the need to experiment, launch, and land new offerings that drive net new revenue.

Google Cloud provides extremely mature security capabilities and solutions to address the needs of today. Whether we're talking about SaaS solutions that joined the Google family through acquisitions (such as Mandiant) or Google Cloud native tooling that helps customers secure their environments (such as Security Command Center), Google Cloud customers will find themselves building infrastructure on one of the most robust and secure platforms in the world.

In the next chapter, we'll learn about IT operations in the cloud with a particular focus on DevOps, SRE, and the importance of service availability for businesses.

11

IT Operations in the Cloud

Building and managing infrastructure in the cloud versus on-premises has implications for how teams are structured and how they operate. This, in turn, has led to the rise of roles and concepts such as **developer operations** (**DevOps**) and **site reliability engineering** (**SRE**). Before we dig into these concepts in this chapter, we'll highlight the main differences between operating cloud environments relative to on-premises.

By the end of this chapter, you will be able to do the following:

- Describe the differences between cloud and self-hosted infrastructure
- Understand DevOps and SRE and how they apply to businesses

This chapter covers the following topics:

- Service availability – on-premises versus cloud
- Overview of DevOps
- SRE and how it applies to business

Service availability – on-premises versus cloud

As covered in previous chapters, operating in a cloud environment has nuances and sometimes can be very different from building and managing your infrastructure in a proprietary data center. When you build your data center infrastructure, you will have to hire for a wide range of skills. Your physical data center and infrastructure team may be as large – if not larger – than your development team.

You'll have to hire folks to work through the real-estate portion of the project, identifying potential geographies for where the data center could be located. Once a location has been established, you may need to build out the data center itself. This would mean construction crews building the warehouse, implementing the appropriate power and cooling systems, and installing the racks that will house the servers. From there, you need to procure hardware and software to be deployed in the data center.

These purchases can be very expensive and time-consuming, given the need to navigate the purchasing process of multiple technology vendors. Assuming your team can do everything mentioned here promptly, it may still take over a year before the data center infrastructure will be ready to use in production.

Once the data center is up and running, you'll need a team to run physical security for your data center, ensuring only folks with the need to access the data center have access to it. You'll also need teams to run the data center infrastructure itself, ensuring that all of the infrastructure is up to date, secured, available, and performant.

In some cases, organizations may opt to use a **colocation (colo)** facility to house their infrastructure. In that circumstance, the colo provider is responsible for most of the physical aspects of the data center, such as power, cooling, and the physical space. The customer of a colocation facility, however, is still responsible for racking their hardware and managing the infrastructure.

Ensuring services are secure, scalable, and available becomes a major challenge and focus for teams running on-premises infrastructure. Uptime and service availability in particular is a focus for data center teams, particularly when the systems are externally facing and their purpose is to serve customers or generate revenue. The way that uptime is measured is by representing the percentage of time across a year that a service is available and functional. This is typically referred to as the number of 9s that reflect the uptime. For example, if a service has *five 9s* of availability, it would be recognized as being up 99.999% of the time. Similarly, if a service has *four 9s* of uptime, then the service is expected to be up 99.99% of the time. Downtime, by contrast, represents how often you'd expect a service to be down.

To add some context to the five 9s and four 9s of uptime, it's helpful to look at how many minutes of downtime the respective systems will have. If a system has 99.999% uptime, it would effectively only be down for 5.26 minutes a year. If a system has 99.99% uptime, however, it would have an order of magnitude more downtime – 52.25 minutes a year.

Whenever you launch an online service, customers will expect a **service-level agreement (SLA)** to represent how reliable the service is. Depending on the use case of the service, customers will expect a system to be more or less reliable. Systems that are intended to be the backbone of revenue-generating workflows may be expected to have 99.999% or 99.995% uptime while systems that are internally facing or not tied to anything that generates revenue may have less stringent requirements, such as 99.95% uptime.

Although the terms uptime and availability are often used interchangeably, there is some nuance related to the two terms. **Uptime** refers specifically to whether or not a system is up and running. It does not take into account things that may impact system performance, such as spikes in usage. **Availability**, however, takes into account variables such as planned maintenance and unscheduled downtime to focus specifically on whether a system is usable.

There are a few different factors that can impact uptime and service availability for technology systems. The way systems are architected, the quality of the hardware and software, and the level of maintenance and support all impact a system's reliability. In addition, factors related to the data center itself can impact uptime, such as power outages, fires, flooding, and, by extension, natural disasters – these can impact service reliability, highlighting the importance of geography when building data centers.

To avoid major issues that can arise from the challenges highlighted previously, infrastructure teams will implement procedures, practices, and technology that drive toward maximizing uptime. As you can imagine, an application that generates revenue through an e-commerce platform would have better customer retention and revenue generation, assuming it has five 9s of uptime rather than four 9s.

A couple of practices that have risen to prominence in recent years have been DevOps and SRE. As technology teams raced to build globally scalable applications and new features while facing pressure from security and compliance teams, DevOps and SRE proved to be great tools for managing competing interests and optimizing teams for these needs of the future. In the next few sections of this chapter, we'll explore the impact they are having on technology teams and architecture and how they can help with designing applications and systems.

Overview of DevOps

Traditionally, infrastructure and development teams were treated as independent functions and there was minimal collaboration between the two. Infrastructure teams were responsible for provisioning and managing infrastructure, while the development team was responsible for building and shipping code. The conflict arose from the fact that the two teams had conflicting mandates. The infrastructure team's responsibility was to maintain the infrastructure operational, while developers wanted to make changes to those systems. Whenever you introduce new code or changes to systems and applications, you are increasing the risk of downtime. This created a culture where infrastructure teams may want to minimize changes and demand a long, rigorous process for changes. Developers, however, needed a way to release software more often while ensuring lower failure rates, faster recovery times, a shorter lead time between fixes, and generally more frequent deployments.

The issue with this is that when you are building a software company, your ability to ship code is directly correlated to your ability to compete. If your competitors, over a year or two, can match your feature set and surpass it, you will have a really hard time staying relevant to your customers. Not only will you struggle to retain customers, but you will also have a hard time attracting new customers.

As these pain points became pointed, a set of practices was developed to build a bridge between infrastructure and software teams. DevOps was able to establish a structure for how the two teams collaborate while also defining best practices for improving outcomes. At its core, DevOps is the push toward automation where the development life cycle is shortened through the adoption of automated testing, configuration, and release management. Teams adopt approaches such as **continuous integration and continuous delivery (CI/CD)**, **Infrastructure as Code (IaC)**, monitoring, and Agile.

By adopting automated testing, deployment, configuration, and management, development teams can account for many of the challenges they face that arise from human error. The adoption of an Agile culture that emphasizes continuous iteration and the breaking down of applications into services and microservices also significantly contributes to the improvement of developer productivity.

An example of how this translates to a cloud environment is how projects are managed at the folder and project level. A development team may have a folder with three subfolders: development, testing, and production. The development environment is the first point of development, where folks explore different services to deliver a specific capability or workflow. Once the development architecture has been established, it is reconstructed in the testing environment. The engineer who does the testing and quality assurance then runs multiple tests to ensure the architecture is viable in production. Assuming all the tests are passed, it is then implemented in production. Similarly, in the world of development, having a structure around dev, test, and production is critical to ensure that only production-grade code will be pushed to the production environment.

The cloud in particular complements the Agile way of developing software because many of the physical limitations of running data centers are abstracted away. Within Google Cloud, for example, getting access to additional machines can be as easy as submitting a quota increase request where the additional hardware is provisioned with minimal effort. If a specific zone is low on resources, projects can be easily spun up in a new region or zone to minimize the impact on developer productivity. It's also easy for infrastructure teams to monitor usage, assign the appropriate permissions, limit the amount of hardware developers have access to, and even set budget alerts to help with financial governance.

Some of the benefits of adopting DevOps include improved customer satisfaction, enhanced productivity, reduced risk in the development life cycle, improved quality, and increased flexibility. That's why many organizations have moved toward the adoption of DevOps and its associated practices. Not only are they able to ship more code faster but the code is of higher quality than it would be otherwise.

Now that we understand the impact DevOps has on development teams, let's explore how SRE has impacted infrastructure teams.

SRE and how it applies to business

SRE is a practice pioneered by Google that implements principles such as automation everywhere, reliability as a core focus, and continuous monitoring in the world of infrastructure. SRE teams adopt many practices similar to DevOps, such as the adoption of automation, testing, and continuous delivery to streamline operations. They collect and analyze data on system health, ensuring that issues are identified before an outage, to maximize uptime. They also design systems from the ground up to be reliable and resilient. This minimizes the impact of outages and can entail the adoption of multi-regional architecture, load balancing traffic, and dynamic scaling of infrastructure across multiple zones based on load. They also focus on and tackle performance issues and improvements so that they have a culture of continuous optimization for their infrastructure.

SRE teams are tasked with collaborating with other teams to strike a balance between reliability and releases. They partner with customers and product teams to define infrastructure metrics relative to uptime and availability. They're also expected to have a holistic view of systems and their relationships, ensuring they can quickly respond to issues when they occur and ideally identify them before a problem occurs at all. This builds rigor in technology teams as they think about and implement practices that will take best practices, automation, and collaboration into account.

For example, the SRE team may partner with the cloud development and security teams to define a set of best practices for infrastructure and have it implemented as templates. The adoption of IaC is also very beneficial to SRE teams as they can help define and standardize templates for supported architectures, network topology, machine types, and operating systems so that teams build exclusively on corporate-approved systems and architectures.

These practices can also be extended to managing permissions, where they can define specific user groups, assign the respective permissions, and define firewall rules and instance makeup in a script so that it can be implemented by the DevOps team or the development team whenever they want to create a new development environment.

There are many advantages to the adoption of SRE, including reduced downtime, improved customer satisfaction, risk minimization, increased agility, and catalyzing innovation. If your service is more reliable than your competitor's, you can frame that as competitive differentiation. By extension, if you have better uptime, then you can generate more revenue or provide a better customer experience.

In addition, through the adoption of SRE practices, your infrastructure team becomes an accelerator of innovation rather than a blocker of it. Where historically they may have been the "no" team, they are given the tools and practices to enable innovation and collaboration throughout the organization.

Summary

Organizations that adopt modern practices for managing development and infrastructure can establish significant competitive advantages over those that don't. Through the adoption of practices such as automation, monitoring, and collaboration, teams are equipped to be as productive as possible while still having controls in place to ensure the quality of the work is also improved.

Now that we understand the impact of adopting DevOps and SRE practices, let's dig into the tooling that's built into Google Cloud to facilitate the adoption of those practices.

12

Resource Monitoring and Application Performance Management on Google Cloud

The previous chapter introduced us to the concepts of DevOps and SRE, highlighting the importance of operational excellence in managing development and technology infrastructure. In this chapter, we'll dig into operationalizing those practices through resource monitoring and application performance management. In addition, we'll highlight the impact of downtime on businesses and explore the Google Cloud-specific tools to address those needs.

By the end of this chapter, you will be able to do the following:

- Describe the impact of outages on customers
- Understand SRE practices and definitions in operating cloud environments
- Describe Google Cloud tools for observability and application performance practices

This chapter covers the following topics:

- Downtime and its impact on business
- Cloud operations – monitoring, logging, and observability
- Google Cloud tools for resource monitoring and maintenance

Downtime and its impact on business

Downtown minimization is at the heart of what many infrastructure teams focus on. Whether you're building out your own data center, working out of a co-location facility, or leveraging a hyperscale cloud such as Google Cloud, one of the key measurements of your team's success is reliability. **Reliability** refers to the ability to provide uninterrupted and performant services to your clients. Improving reliability is something that can be achieved through several strategies and at different levels of the architecture.

Redundancy is a key concept in ensuring systems are reliable. **Redundancy** refers to running infrastructure and systems in a way that even if systems fail, there is minimal disruption or no disruption at all to the customer experience. This is achieved by duplicating systems to provide an alternative should the primary system(s) fail. This may mean duplicating an entire data center or deployment so that outages have minimal impact on clients.

As you can imagine, replicating entire environments for the sake of redundancy can be extremely expensive. Businesses need to have meaningful arguments to justify such massive capital investments. That begs the question – why would someone spend that much money on minimizing downtime? The answer is that the impact of a major outage or service disruption could end up costing significantly more than the technology and skills investment.

Imagine that you work at a bank and one of your major clients decides to travel to Tokyo for a business meeting. While in Tokyo, there is an emergency and they need to execute a transfer from their bank account to handle it. They pull up your mobile app on their phone to access their account and… the app is inaccessible. It turns out that the data center hosting the application had an outage and your infrastructure teams hadn't architected the infrastructure to be redundant and reliable. This impacts your client's ability to handle the emergency and they are left with a bad taste in their mouth over the experience. They end up deciding to switch banks in the hopes of finding one that has better technology infrastructure to support Asia. Assuming this client has millions in funds with the bank, the lack of reliable systems costs the bank the client and their millions in funds.

In an even more extreme scenario, what if the customer was a hospital system? What if a doctor was trying to access patient records during a medical emergency to validate whether the patient has any allergies? Lack of access to a critical system during an emergency can have significant, negative consequences. The doctor could end up using a treatment that triggers an even more violent medical issue with the patient.

Organizations that work with regulated industries or support business-critical systems have the responsibility of ensuring that systems are accessible at all times. Outages can cost millions of dollars to clients and even cause irreparable damage, depending on the circumstances. Now that we understand the importance of having reliable infrastructure, let's explore some of the business benefits:

- Customer satisfaction and trust
- Improved operational efficiency
- Resilience

Let's look at them in detail.

Customer satisfaction and trust

Customers can be extremely demanding when making technology decisions. It can take years to build a good reputation and one major outage to ruin it. Depending on the customer, they may need to run business-critical systems that are directly linked to financial transactions, government decision making, or even saving lives. If the systems require 99.995% or 99.999% uptime, customers will require the provider to deliver this level of service consistently and often request **service-level agreements** (**SLAs**) in writing before moving forward with a purchase.

SLAs outline a provider's commitment to a certain level of service performance and quality, and a designation of responsibilities, as defined by a contractual obligation to their clients. By establishing SLAs and living up to their expectations, organizations can win customers in the long run by ensuring that they are happy and trust their technology decisions. This helps with client retention and even upselling them to other services that you may offer.

Improved operational efficiency

Human and machine errors are bound to happen eventually and designing systems for resilience ensures that there are policies, tools, and people in place to handle these issues when they occur. By incorporating DevOps and SRE practices into infrastructure teams, you can ensure that teams are building applications with agility, security, and reliability in mind. Decisions are taken to introduce automation and **infrastructure as code** (**IaC**), among other strategies that streamline productivity and increase the reliability of systems, even during outages or major code pushes.

This operational excellence will pay dividends by freeing up engineering resources that would normally be dedicated to managing infrastructure to focus on other, more valuable tasks. For example, database administrators can transition to becoming data engineers, helping data science and AI teams architect their data pipelines. Work that was normally dedicated to a human being is automated through code, such as running tests and having visibility into system health in real time.

Resilience

Businesses that adopt a mindset of building highly scalable, redundant, available, and secure systems can also achieve resilience in serving their customers. Assuming there are challenges such as networking outages, hardware failures, or even natural disasters, the systems are designed in a way that these issues will not have a major impact on the customer experience.

Through resilience, organizations can build a competitive advantage and outclass the competition when working with clients that require strict SLA adherence and highly available systems. Resilience also builds a culture of problem-solving, contingency planning, and continuous improvement, which are critical to establishing long-term success in the technology industry.

Now that we understand the importance of reliability and its impact on businesses earning and retaining customers, let's explore the tooling available on Google Cloud to help establish operational excellence within cloud infrastructure and development teams.

Cloud operations – monitoring, logging, and observability

When building out a cloud environment, it's important to implement the operational best practices described in this book. This includes building an organizational structure that incorporates DevOps, SRE, and security best practices. What this looks like in practice is the implementation of strong **identity and access management** (**IAM**) practices and segmenting development, test, and production environments. Depending on the use case for the application, this also means architecting systems to be multi-regional, which strengthens their resilience across reliability, availability, and fault tolerance.

Regarding IAM, within Google Cloud, it's important to remember that everything has an identity – even infrastructure. Google Cloud manages permissions through identities, so resources must also have an identity to have permissions assigned to them. Resources within Google Cloud, such as an instance running in Compute Engine, can be assigned what's called a **service account**. Service accounts allow infrastructure to authenticate and have access to resources through permissions associated with the service account.

For example, an application may need to make an API call to an internal or external system to process a specific request. To ensure this isn't abused by malicious actors, you typically want this permission to be as restrictive as possible, only allowing communication between your application and approved systems. IAM and service accounts give you the tools through which to restrict with whom your resources can interface based on a set of permissions that can be managed centrally.

Another best practice as it relates to IAM and security is the management of permissions at the group level. Whenever defining user roles and permissions, this should always be defined in groups rather than on an individual basis. If permissions are assigned on an individual level, it can be very easy to over-provision access and difficult to manage at scale. By defining user roles and groups, with the associated permissions, you can quickly and easily remove users and service accounts from groups to update permissions over time. If someone switches from the development team to the AI team, they would need to have their permissions updated. They may need to be removed from being able to push code to the testing or production environments while being granted access to data warehousing and data science projects. While this may seem trivial for one person, imagine an organization with hundreds – if not thousands – of employees on technology teams.

This can also be extrapolated to service accounts, where you may have a different set of permissions for your development environment versus your production environment. Within a development environment, you may only want services to access historical data from a data warehouse or some sort of static dataset. In a production environment, by contrast, you may want to have your services fetch data from a production database to serve it directly to clients.

Beyond being able to track who does what in your environment, it's also important to understand where and how things fail. Systems and people are not perfect and they are bound to go down eventually. To be able to quickly identify issues and remedy them, it's important to have visibility into your environment. This includes having visibility into the operational health of machines, networking traffic, and tracking all of this information.

To build a successful cloud operations team, you must have a way of understanding your environment and the root cause when things go wrong. By implementing tools that provide observability and logging, the operations team will have the information that they need to properly assess the situation when issues arise and move quickly to fix issues.

Monitoring tools can collect data from your infrastructure, such as health metrics, events, and metadata, giving you real-time visibility into the health of your systems. More advanced systems are even able to help identify issues when they arise, trigger alerts, and kick off automated resolution. This visibility helps you understand how your systems are performing, measure their availability, and identify potential health issues. If your database's resources, such as CPU or RAM, are running consistently at 80%-100% utilization, odds are there may be performance degradation for customers. In this case, you should look at either increasing the hardware to handle the load or potentially creating a read replica to offload some of the traffic from the main database.

Logging is also an important component of being able to triage issues when they occur. Having monitoring tools in real time is valuable but if you need to conduct an investigation over several days, weeks, or even months, having a central repository of your logs that you can quickly access and navigate is tremendously important. Logging provides a detailed record of activities, such as system access, behavior, actions, interactions, and system events.

Observability practices build on top of monitoring and logging by focusing on establishing a deeper understanding of the relationship between systems and how they interact. Tracing, for example, is a technique where you track the flow of information or requests across a complex system to identify dependencies and uncover the root cause of issues that may arise from an outage or performance degradation.

By implementing monitoring, logging, and observability practices, technology and infrastructure teams can establish a strong operational posture. This will enable them to respond quickly to issues, identify them before they occur, and deliver an excellent customer experience. Their systems will be consistently healthy, available, and reliable. Issues will be troubleshot quickly and remediation will be implemented with a high degree of confidence so that the root cause will be addressed. In addition, resource utilization will be optimized, with the dynamic right-sizing of infrastructure based on traffic patterns as they will be more in tune with the nuances of the traffic patterns of different systems. Lastly, they will also be able to ensure the appropriate security and compliance practices are implemented as they will have an understanding of whether or not their systems are compliant and address issues as they arise in real time.

Let's explore the tooling available in Google Cloud to help with observability practices.

Google Cloud tools for resource monitoring and maintenance

Earlier in this chapter, we established the importance of visibility, monitoring, and observability for infrastructure teams. Without information related to system health, performance, and relationships, it can be extremely challenging to resolve technical issues. Let's assume an organization would like to implement those practices – where should they start? The good news is that there is tooling built into Google Cloud to help organizations gain visibility and collect logs from their environment.

The **Cloud Monitoring** tool in Google Cloud provides clients with the visibility they need to understand their systems' performance, health, and availability. Cloud Monitoring can collect data from systems such as metrics, events, and metadata. This data collection is supported for Google Cloud, **Amazon Web Services** (**AWS**), application instruments, and hosted uptime probes. You can also extend Cloud Monitoring's capabilities to on-premises systems, hybrid systems, and 50+ common application components through **BindPlane**, a third-party tool built by observIQ.

Cloud Monitoring provides value to clients by offering automatic, out-of-the-box metrics collection and pre-built dashboards. This helps infrastructure teams establish a strong observability foundation when getting started with Google Cloud and reduces the manual toil of having to set up all of the tooling. Having one central monitoring system significantly reduces the complexity and overhead of running a mature observability practice. One central service collects all of the logs across service metrics, uptime monitoring, and dashboarding and kicks off remediation workflows such as alerting.

When discussing the process of monitoring services and applications, it's important to highlight the difference between SLAs, **service-level objectives** (**SLOs**), and **service-level indicators** (**SLIs**). As highlighted in *Chapter 11*, SLAs are commitments that technology companies make to their clients related to the uptime and availability of their systems. They're a contractual obligation and, as such, are communicated directly to the client as a commitment through contractual language. SLAs are externally facing and meant to establish an externally facing expectation.

Technology and infrastructure teams are tasked with ensuring that systems and applications live up to the expectations set within the customer contract as an SLA. This is defined internally as an SLO, which is a statement of the expected level of performance for a system. To measure adherence to SLOs, SLIs are defined, which are the metrics through which uptime and availability are measured. By defining and tracking the appropriate metrics, infrastructure teams can ensure that systems are compliant with the SLAs that are defined in customer contracts and their internal SLOs.

Now that we understand how SRE is implemented through observability practices, let's explore some of the features of the Google Cloud Monitoring service:

- **SLO monitoring**: Cloud Monitoring helps organizations live up to their SLAs by having them implement SLIs and SLOs, ensuring that systems are in compliance with customer expectations and that actions are taken when service health or reliability is degraded.

- **Managed Prometheus and Ops Agent**: Cloud Monitoring includes a managed service for **Prometheus**, a tool that's used in Kubernetes for the simplification of log and metrics collection, storage, and analysis. **Ops Agent** provides logging and metrics collection through a unified endpoint agent that can be deployed on **virtual machines** (**VMs**) and managed at scale with popular tools.

- **Native Google Cloud integration**: Cloud Monitoring has been integrated with Google Cloud and its console to be able to monitor all resources and services with no additional instrumentation.

By having visibility into their environment and implementing the appropriate controls, infrastructure teams can ensure that their systems are healthy and performant. Having a mature operations team that leverages SRE practices will ensure that customers aren't impacted by outages that can be easily avoided, retaining their trust and their business. Google Cloud offers GCP-native tooling and a marketplace of ISV solutions for customers to implement what makes sense for them as it relates to expertise, cost, and compliance requirements. Infrastructure that is built on Google Cloud benefits from Google's SRE practices, allowing customers to build highly reliable, resilient, and scalable systems with relative ease.

Summary

To establish and retain customer trust, organizations need to ensure that their technology teams operate with operational excellence and best practices in mind. This includes incorporating DevOps and SRE methodologies where relevant to maximize productivity while also reducing risk and error.

Google Cloud is greatly positioned to enable these practices, not only because there is tooling built into the platform to help adhere to these practices but also because Google pioneered both DevOps and SRE. This means that open source projects such as Istio and Prometheus are adopted quickly and provided as managed services on the platform and that Google will build native tooling to facilitate running environments with excellence.

The *Google Cloud Digital Leader* certification is a great stepping stone into both the Google ecosystem and more generally the cloud space. It is built on a foundation of practices pioneered by Google across topics such as DevOps, SRE, machine learning, and big data. The cloud space is evolving from an infrastructure-focused business to helping folks derive value from data. To monetize data, organizations need to ensure that data is properly procured, stored, secured, and processed as per best practices and compliance requirements.

In the next chapter, we will surface a series of test questions to help you prepare for the exam. When thinking about your responses, think about the business challenges that are being solved through technology. Take your time reading the question, thinking through the options, and landing on the final answer through the process of elimination.

The test will include questions that are either definition-centric or situational, ensuring that you are familiar with the most common services used in Google Cloud and their functions, as well as what problems they address for customers. They are made up of 100 multiple choice questions and test takers have 90 minutes to complete them. Google offers both virtual and in-person testing options for test takers.

Part 5:
Practice Exam Questions

The fifth and last part of this book will have 100 practice test questions to help you prepare to certify as a Google Cloud Digital Leader. It is composed of both terminology and situational questions, helping you validate that you can describe key terms and concepts before taking the exam. The situational questions will help with critical thinking as you work through a specific situation and provide the best answer given the circumstances.

This part has the following chapter:

- *Chapter 13, Sample Questions: Exam Preparation*

13
Sample Questions: Exam Preparation

The **Google Cloud Digital Leader certification** is a great certification for folks who are new to Google Cloud and, more generally, the cloud space. It provides a foundational understanding of the industry, highlighting core concepts for why the cloud is valuable and the strategic business reasons a company would adopt it.

The exam itself will be composed of 50 to 60 exam questions, all multiple choice, and the test taker will be tasked with responding with the best answer given the scenario. Some questions may be more straightforward, such as identifying the correct definition for a specific term, or more complex, such as where there may be multiple correct answers but you must find the *best* answer.

In this section of the exam guide, you will be provided with 100 sample questions to help you understand the format and types of questions you will be asked on the exam. These questions may not exactly match the exam questions, but they are designed to help you think through the subject matter of this book and be prepared to take the real exam.

The real exam will have roughly four sections, with the subject matter being broken down into the following coverage areas:

- **10%**: Digital transformation on Google Cloud
- **30%**: Data innovation on Google Cloud
- **30%**: Application and infrastructure modernization on Google Cloud
- **30%**: Cloud security and operations on Google Cloud

The following practice questions are intended to help you start thinking through the types of questions and answers you'll run into on the exam. For more details on the exam itself, feel free to visit https://cloud.google.com/learn/certification/guides/cloud-digital-leader.

The following practice questions will be broken down into three sections:

- A 20-question pop quiz

  - Fundamental cloud concepts in a simple format

- A 60-question product quiz

  - Google Cloud-specific product questions

- A 20-question situational quiz

  - Scenario-based questions where you pick the best answer based on the options

Part 1 – 20-question "pop quiz" – digital transformation on Google Cloud

1. What is cloud infrastructure?

   A. A way to virtually host servers and applications.

   B. An airborne hosting method.

   C. Software as a service.

   D. A submerged data center.

2. Which of the following is NOT a benefit to hosting infrastructure in the cloud?

   A. Scalability.

   B. Agility.

   C. Control.

   D. Flexibility.

3. Why do businesses move from on-premises environments to the cloud?

   A. Shared responsibility model.

   B. They want more control over their hardware and software.

   C. Both.

   D. None of the above.

4. What is one of the benefits of the shared responsibility model?

    A. They control the entire technology stack.

    B. It empowers IT teams to manage and control more hardware decisions.

    C. It offloads security responsibilities to a third party.

    D. None of the above.

5. What does IaaS stand for?

    A. Institution as a Service.

    B. Information as a Service.

    C. Invention as a Service.

    D. Infrastructure as a Service.

6. What is **Software as a Service (SaaS)**?

    A. When an application is delivered directly to end users over the internet.

    B. When an application with platform tooling is delivered to builders.

    C. When virtualization is provided to infrastructure teams as a service.

    D. None of the above.

7. What is the difference between the private and public cloud?

    A. There is no difference between them.

    B. The private cloud is dedicated to one organization while the public cloud is shared between multiple organizations.

    C. The public cloud is dedicated to one organization while the private cloud is shared between multiple organizations.

    D. None of the above.

8. What is a hybrid environment?

    A. When an organization leverages two or more cloud infrastructure providers.

    B. When an organization hosts its infrastructure on-premises.

    C. When an organization has both on-premises and cloud infrastructure.

    D. None of the above.

9. What is a multi-cloud environment?

    A. When an organization hosts its infrastructure on-premises.

    B. When an organization leverages one cloud provider and on-premises infrastructure.

    C. When an organization leverages only SaaS solutions.

    D. None of the above.

10. What are some of the main benefits of building and transforming infrastructure on Google Cloud?

    A. Intelligence.

    B. Collaboration.

    C. Trust.

    D. All of the above.

11. You head the technology team of a traditional company. You have some data and systems that need to stay on-premises but you'd like to also take advantage of innovation in the cloud. What type of environment would you recommend to your CEO?

    A. Cloud only.

    B. Hybrid.

    C. Multi-cloud.

    D. None of the above.

12. You are the CTO for a newly built start-up. You'd like to build a company that fully leverages the benefits of the cloud. What type of environment and technologies do you recommend to your CEO?

    A. Hybrid, traditional.

    B. Cloud, cloud-native.

    C. Cloud, traditional.

    D. None of the above.

13. Why would a traditional organization decide to maintain some infrastructure on-premises?

    A. Contractual obligations.

    B. Compliance requirements.

    C. Legacy hardware requirements.

    D. All of the above.

14. What does TCO refer to in regard to technology infrastructure and related business decisions?

    A. Total cost of ownership.

    B. Total cloud ownership.

    C. Technology cloud ownership.

    D. None of the above.

15. How does Google Cloud define its data centers?

    A. Regions and zones, with each region having multiple zones.

    B. Zones and regions, with each zone having multiple regions.

    C. Locations and points of presence, with each location having multiple points of presence.

    D. Points of presence and locations, with each point of presence having multiple locations.

16. What is the function of a **Domain Name Server (DNS)**?

    A. To protect web applications and services from **denial-of-service (DDoS)** attacks.

    B. To load balance traffic across multiple endpoints.

    C. To translate websites into IP addresses and route the traffic accordingly.

    D. None of the above.

17. Google Cloud is built on top of Google's global, proprietary network, allowing it to ensure that all traffic is encrypted at rest and in transit by default.

    A. True.

    B. False.

18. Within the SaaS model of software deployment and hosting, who is responsible for managing users and data?

    A. The customer.

    B. The SaaS provider.

    C. Both.

    D. Neither.

19. Within the **Platform as a Service (PaaS)** model of software deployment, who is responsible for patching and managing virtual machines and their associated operating systems?

    A. The customer.

    B. The PaaS provider.

C. Both.

D. Neither.

20. Within the **Infrastructure as a Service (IaaS)** model of software deployment, who is responsible for patching and managing virtual machines and their associated operating systems?

A. The customer.

B. The IaaS provider.

C. Both.

D. Neither.

Part 2 – 60-question "product quiz" – data, infrastructure, AppMod, Security, and CloudOps

1. What is Google Cloud's first-party data ingestion tool?

A. Managed Kafka.

B. Pub/Sub.

C. Managed Airflow.

D. Dataflow.

2. What service does Google Cloud recommend as the foundation for building a data lake?

A. Cloud Storage.

B. BigQuery.

C. Bigtable.

D. Dataproc.

3. What Google Cloud service helps with metadata mapping, search, and data ownership in data lakes?

A. Dataproc.

B. Dataflow.

C. BigQuery.

D. Data Catalog.

4. What mature data visualization tool does Google Cloud offer as a first-party subscription?

    A. Tableau.

    B. Data Studio.

    C. Plotly.

    D. Looker.

5. What is Dataflow?

    A. A data visualization tool with an HBase **software development kit (SDK)**.

    B. A data visualization tool with an Apache Beam SDK.

    C. A data transformation tool with an HBase SDK.

    D. A data transformation tool with an Apache Beam SDK.

6. What is Google Cloud's first-party data warehouse solution?

    A. Bigtable.

    B. Druid.

    C. BigQuery.

    D. Snowflake.

7. What is Google Cloud's first-party MLOps platform called?

    A. Vertex AI Platform.

    B. Vector ML Platform.

    C. Virtual Brain Platform.

    D. Bedrock.

8. What are Google's biggest strengths in AI/ML?

    A. Google employs 3,000+ AI researchers.

    B. Google has published 7,000+ AI research papers.

    C. Google pioneered MLOps as a practice.

    D. All of the above.

9. What is Google's approach to AI tooling and services?

    A. Target users with productivity solutions such as Duet AI for Workspace.

    B. Target builders and developers with solutions such as the Vertex AI Platform.

    C.   Target infrastructure folks with AI-optimized hardware.

    D.   All of the above.

10. What open source project does Dataproc provide as a managed service?

    A.   Apache Beam.

    B.   Apache Spark.

    C.   Apache Hive.

    D.   None of the above.

11. What databases does Google Cloud's Cloud SQL support?

    A.   Microsoft SQL Server.

    B.   MySQL.

    C.   PostgreSQL.

    D.   All of the above.

12. Which of the following is NOT a first-party data product for Google Cloud?

    A.   BigQuery.

    B.   Bigtable.

    C.   Snowflake.

    D.   Looker.

13. What are the Google-managed options for **extract, transform, and load** (ETL) on Google Cloud?

    A.   Dataflow.

    B.   Dataproc.

    C.   Datadog.

    D.   A and B.

14. What is Google Cloud's horizontally scalable relational database?

    A.   Spanner.

    B.   CloudSQL.

    C.   All of the above.

    D.   None of the above.

15. Why is BigQuery different from other traditional data warehouses?

   A. The compute and storage are decoupled.

   B. The compute can scale dynamically based on the query.

   C. The storage can scale dynamically based on the volume of data.

   D. All of the above.

16. You are a data scientist who wants to start playing with data and experimenting with **machine learning (ML)**. You have some experience with Jupyter and Colab notebooks. What Google Cloud service would be helpful?

   A. Cloud Shell.

   B. Vertex AI Notebooks.

   C. Looker.

   D. Spanner.

17. You are an IT director who wants to free up your database team who are using MySQL to work on more meaningful projects such as building a data lake. What Google Cloud service would best suit you given the circumstances?

   A. Compute Engine.

   B. Spanner.

   C. BigQuery.

   D. CloudSQL.

18. You are an ML specialist who is using BigQuery. You want to do some simple ML based on the dataset you have in the warehouse. What is the easiest way to run inference on your data?

   A. Leverage the Vertex AI platform.

   B. Leverage BigQuery's native ML capability – BQML.

   C. Export the data to an on-premises ML model training and serving solution.

   D. None of the above.

19. You are an ML specialist who has a dataset with customer and support rep conversations. You'd like to get a sense of customer sentiment based on the words used during the interactions. What Google Cloud ML API would help you?

   A. **Natural Language Processing (NLP)**.

   B. Image Analysis.

    C.   Video Analysis.

    D.   PaLM2 Chat.

20. You are an ML specialist who would like to prototype an information bot. Which Google Cloud solution should you use?

    A.   Google Workspace's Duet AI.

    B.   Google Cloud's Duet AI.

    C.   Vertex Search and Conversation.

    D.   Bard.

21. What is Google Cloud's **virtual machine (VM)** hosting service called?

    A.   Google Cloud Virtual Machines.

    B.   Google Cloud Compute Machines.

    C.   Google Cloud Virtual Engine.

    D.   Google Cloud Compute Engine.

22. What are **Managed Instance Groups (MIGs)**?

    A.   A VM deployment pipeline.

    B.   A service that allows for the number of VMs to scale up and down based on load.

    C.   A service that allows the hardware allocated to a VM to scale up and down based on load.

    D.   None of the above.

23. What is Google Cloud's first-party solution that can be used to decouple services from a legacy application without meaningful transformation to the application's code?

    A.   Compute Engine.

    B.   Kubernetes Engine.

    C.   Apigee.

    D.   None of the above.

24. What is **Google Kubernetes Engine (GKE)**?

    A.   Google Cloud delivering managed Borg as a service to customers.

    B.   Google Cloud delivering managed Functions as a service to customers.

    C.   Google Cloud delivering managed AI as a service to customers.

    D.   Google Cloud delivering managed Kubernetes as a service to customers.

25. What are some of GKE's key features?

    A. Serverless with Autopilot.

    B. Pod and cluster Autoscaling.

    C. A and B.

    D. None of the above.

26. What are some of the drivers for modernizing applications?

    A. Improving reliability.

    B. Improving scalability.

    C. Improving performance.

    D. All of the above.

27. Which of the following is/are a benefit of leveraging cloud-native applications?

    A. Leverage real-time data to drive better decisions.

    B. Having full control over the infrastructure, software, and hardware decisions.

    C. Develop new monetization streams.

    D. A and C.

28. What are some of the challenges facing traditional organizations trying to leverage data?

    A. Data siloes.

    B. Security restrictions.

    C. Compliance restrictions.

    D. All of the above.

29. What is Google Cloud's service for serverless application hosting, without the need to containerize applications or launch them via VMs?

    A. App Engine.

    B. Compute Engine.

    C. Kubernetes Engine.

    D. Cloud Run.

30. What is Google Cloud's service for serverless hosting of containers and functions?

    A. App Engine.

    B. Compute Engine.

    C. Kubernetes Engine.

    D. Cloud Run.

31. Beyond decoupling services from monolithic applications, what value does Apigee provide?

    A. An enterprise-grade way of managing permissions and access to data for external customers and partners.

    B. A submerged data center for HPC workloads.

    C. A satellite network for streaming distributed data.

    D. None of the above.

32. You have a containerized workload you want to deploy. You would like for it to autoscale but need to be able to have granular control over traffic routing, security controls, and the OS for the nodes. Which solution should you use?

    A. App Engine.

    B. Compute Engine.

    C. Kubernetes Engine.

    D. Cloud Run.

33. You have a VM-based workload you would like to deploy. Which solution should you use?

    A. App Engine.

    B. Compute Engine.

    C. Kubernetes Engine.

    D. Cloud Run.

34. You work for a mobile gaming company. Your company is moving out of a traditional data center and your main game is a monolithic application. You'd like to be able to do things such as canary deployments and traffic splitting to enable A/B testing for different game versions. Which GCP service makes the most sense for you?

    A. App Engine.

    B. Compute Engine.

    C. Kubernetes Engine.

    D. Cloud Run.

35. You are building your first start-up. You'd like to implement best practices such as DevOps and a microservice-based architecture, although you don't have a big team or experience managing Kubernetes. What is the best hosting service for you?

    A. App Engine.

    B. Compute Engine.

    C. Kubernetes Engine.

    D. Cloud Run.

36. You are migrating some functions from AWS Lambda. You would like to leverage a service that is optimized for running functions specifically. What is the most appropriate **Google Cloud Platform (GCP)** service for your use case?

    A. Cloud Functions.

    B. Cloud Run.

    C. Compute Engine.

    D. Kubernetes Engine.

37. You are migrating databases from a Microsoft ecosystem to Google Cloud. You would prefer to manage the underlying infrastructure. What GCP service is the most relevant?

    A. Compute Engine.

    B. CloudSQL.

    C. Spanner.

    D. None of the above.

38. You want to migrate infrastructure to Google Cloud with minimal changes. What is the appropriate migration approach?

    A. Lift and shift.

    B. Transform then shift.

    C. Shift then transform.

    D. Rebuild from scratch.

39. You are in the middle of migrating an application from .NET to .NET Core. What is the appropriate migration strategy?

    A. Lift and shift.

    B. Transform then shift.

C. Shift then transform.

D. Rebuild from scratch.

40. What is the shared responsibility model?

A. A way to define who is responsible for what part of the technology stack when leveraging cloud providers.

B. A set of shared responsibilities as defined by the cloud provider and customer.

C. Google's vision for the future of security and cloud relationships.

D. None of the above.

41. What is uptime?

A. A measure of how often an application hits peak usage.

B. A measure of how few users use an application.

C. A measure of how often a system goes down.

D. A measure of how often a system is up and running.

42. What is availability?

A. A measure of how often an application hits peak usage.

B. A measure of how often a system is reachable and usable.

C. A measure of how often a system goes down.

D. A measure of how often a system is up and running.

43. What is the accurate, numerical representation of "five nines"?

A. 9,999.9%.

B. 999.99%.

C. 99.999%.

D. 9.9999%.

44. Roughly how many minutes of downtime per year does someone with "five nines" SLA experience?

A. 50 seconds.

B. Five minutes.

C. 50 minutes.

D. Five hours.

45. Roughly how many minutes of downtime per year does someone with "four nines" SLA experience?

    A. 50 seconds.

    B. Five minutes.

    C. 50 minutes.

    D. Five hours.

46. What is phishing?

    A. When an attacker copies legitimate artifacts to try and trick someone into divulging secrets via the web or email.

    B. When an attacker tries to break into a physical location.

    C. When an attacker uses satellites to sniff communications.

    D. None of the above.

47. What kinds of threats do security teams need to be aware of?

    A. Nation-state attackers.

    B. Insider threats.

    C. Opportunistic attackers.

    D. All of the above.

48. What is an SLA?

    A. A contractual obligation setting service standards such as a level of uptime and reliability to customers.

    B. An internal goal for designating a target level of uptime and reliability.

    C. An internal metric used to measure progress toward a designated uptime goal.

    D. None of the above.

49. What is an SLI?

    A. A contractual obligation designating a level of uptime and reliability to customers.

    B. An internal goal for designating a target level of uptime and reliability.

    C. A technical metric used to measure progress toward a designated SLO goal.

    D. None of the above.

50. What is an SLO?

    A. A contractual obligation designating a level of uptime and reliability to customers.

    B. A goal for designating a target level of uptime and reliability.

    C. An internal metric used to measure progress toward a designated uptime goal.

    D. None of the above.

51. What is the value of DevOps?

    A. It defines a set of practices for maximizing service reliability.

    B. It defines a set of practices for managing ML models and their life cycle.

    C. It defines a set of practices for data monetization.

    D. It defines a set of practices for maximizing developer productivity and streamlining operations.

52. What is the value of **site reliability engineering (SRE)**?

    A. It defines a set of practices for maximizing service reliability.

    B. It defines a set of practices for managing ML models and their lifecycle.

    C. It defines a set of practices for data monetization.

    D. It defines a set of practices for maximizing developer productivity.

53. What is the value of observability in the cloud?

    A. It empowers you to monetize data.

    B. It simplifies the training for ML models.

    C. It provides data and metrics for measuring system health and performance.

    D. None of the above.

54. What tool can Google Cloud customers use for observability?

    A. Cloud Functions.

    B. Apache Airflow.

    C. SaaS.

    D. Cloud Monitoring.

55. How do you assign permissions to infrastructure on Google Cloud?

    A. Create a user account and assign it to a machine.

    B. Service account.

C. You can't assign permissions to infrastructure.

D. None of the above.

56. What is the organizational hierarchy for Google Cloud environments?

A. Org > Folder > Resource > Project.

B. Org > Project > Resource Folder.

C. Org > Folder > Project > Resource.

D. Folder > Org > Project Resource.

57. You are in charge of security and compliance for a start-up in the healthcare space. You would like to leverage a Google Cloud first-party tool to help manage your environment's compliance posture. What Google Cloud service would be helpful?

A. Apigee.

B. Compliance Assessment Service.

C. Compute Engine.

D. Security and Command Center.

58. What is the Titan Security Chip?

A. A malware identification and blocking engine.

B. A way for Google to do **multi-factor authentication (MFA)** on server-side infrastructure.

C. SaaS.

D. A submerged data center.

59. Which of the following is NOT one of the three factors when dealing with authentication?

A. Something you know.

B. Something you are.

C. Something you ask.

D. Something you have.

60. When implementing environment segmentation as a part of DevOps, which environments should you have segregated?

A. Development.

B. Testing.

C. Production.

D. All of the above.

Part 3 – 20 situational questions – questions from all sections

We have two scenarios in this section.

Scenario 1 – E-Commerce

You are the IT Director for an e-commerce company. Historically all of your infrastructure has been deployed on-premises and you are dealing with some legacy infrastructure. Thanks to some work done by your coworkers, your application is already broken down into a few different services. You are currently hosting a self-managed Kubernetes cluster that can't scale beyond the on-premises environment. You also have some services that you are running as functions. The team would like to offload infrastructure management in order to focus on other projects such as security and reliability.

On the data side of the house, you manage a few databases across open source offerings such as MySQL and PostgreSQL. You leverage **customer relationship management** (**CRM**) and marketing platforms to handle sales and marketing campaign information. The team also leverages Redis for caching and has not yet built a data lake or a data warehouse. You've started playing with Apache Spark as your ETL tool and plan to keep using it given that you've already scripted several transformations.

Your executives are asking that you leverage marketing data, sales data, and surveys in order to provide personalized recommendations. These systems are currently siloed from each other and you'll need a way to unify them in order to build the recommendations and make the appropriate predictions.

Based on the preceding scenario, answer the following questions:

1. What is the value of your organization moving to the cloud?

    A. Cost optimization.

    B. Scalability.

    C. Data monetization.

    D. All of the above.

2. Which application hosting service would you recommend to host your infrastructure?

    A. App Engine.

    B. Compute Engine.

    C. Kubernetes Engine.

    D. Cloud Run.

3. What is the value for your team in moving from self-hosted to managed services?

    A. Reduce headcount.

    B. Reallocate resources.

    C. Generate revenue.

    D. Reduce costs.

4. What Google Cloud service would you recommend for hosting the databases?

    A. Spanner.

    B. Firestore.

    C. CloudSQL.

    D. Bigtable.

5. What should be implemented as a raw datastore for unifying data from across the disparate systems?

    A. CloudSQL as a data lake.

    B. Cloud Storage as a data lake.

    C. Vertex AI as a data lake.

    D. None of the above.

6. Which ETL service would you recommend based on your usage of Apache Spark?

    A. Dataproc.

    B. Dataflow.

    C. Dataprep.

    D. None of the above.

7. What Google Cloud service would you recommend as a data warehouse?

    A. Cloud Storage.

    B. CloudSQL.

    C. Bigtable.

    D. BigQuery.

8. You want to train ML models based on your data. What are your options on Google Cloud?

    A. Use BQML to train models and run inference from the warehouse.

    B. Use the Vertex AI platform to train custom models and run inference.

C. A and B.

D. None of the above.

9. You'd like to train a model that can track inventory in real time based on the video feed from a camera. Which AI API would be the most relevant?

A. Natural Language.

B. Vision/Video.

C. Speech to Text / Text to Speech.

D. None of the above.

10. You would like to do sentiment analysis based on customer surveys and product reviews. Which AI API would be the most relevant?

A. Natural Language.

B. Vision/Video.

C. Speech to Text / Text to Speech.

D. None of the above.

Scenario 2 – Healthcare

You are the chief data officer for a healthcare software company. Your organization helps customers understand, explore, and build value on top of their data via your platform. At a high level, your platform is quite functional but there are some inefficiencies that need to be addressed.

You'd like a way to more confidently share data with your partners and customers without having to make major changes to your platform. This will enable new monetization use cases and allow you to be more innovative in the services that you offer. You're also working with your infrastructure team to migrate off a legacy data warehouse, which was creating cost and performance bottlenecks for the team.

In particular, you have a database that retains time series data from patients using health hardware such as a pacemaker or a watch which tracks their biometrics. One of your research teams is asking that we track this data in real time to identify potential health signals that may point to the need for some sort of preventative service. This system services a large set of users, all of which may have multiple devices, and you need some sort of highly scalable and available system to house that data.

When you think about new ways to monetize data, you want to take advantage of the innovation happening in AI and in particular generative AI. You'd like to identify a partner who provides both a robust security posture and strong legal protection assuming an issue does arise.

Based on the preceding scenario, answer the following questions:

1. What is the most relevant compliance legislation for your industry?

    A. PII.

    B. PCI-DSS.

    C. SOC 2.

    D. HIPAA.

2. Which Google Cloud solution gives you granular control over sharing data externally through APIs, minimizing the risk associated with monetizing data?

    A. App Engine.

    B. Apigee.

    C. Kubernetes Engine.

    D. Looker.

3. Which Google Cloud solution is great in real-time time series data on a large scale?

    A. Firestore.

    B. Bigtable.

    C. BigQuery.

    D. None of the above.

4. Which of the following statements is TRUE about Google Cloud?

    A. Google Cloud does not offer indemnification for those using its first-party generative model.

    B. No cloud providers offer indemnification for using their ML models.

    C. Google Cloud offers indemnification for those using their first-party models.

    D. None of the above.

5. Which of the following statements is TRUE about Google Cloud?

    A. Google Cloud does not review nor retain customer prompts and responses.

    B. All cloud providers do not review nor retain customer prompts and responses.

    C. Google Cloud reviews and retains customer prompts and responses.

    D. None of the above.

6. Which Google Cloud service provides an enterprise-grade platform for managing the full life cycle of ML models?

   A. Vertex AI platform.

   B. Bard.

   C. ChatGPT.

   D. Google Search.

7. One of the use cases for your healthcare customers includes transcribing audio files from doctor visits. Which is the appropriate ML API?

   A. Vision/Video.

   B. Natural Language.

   C. Generative.

   D. Speech to Text.

8. Which of the following is NOT a Google first-party generative AI foundation model?

   A. Imagen.

   B. Codey.

   C. Claude.

   D. PaLM.

9. You'd like to ensure that any applications you deploy on Google Cloud will have advanced security capabilities, including DDoS protection. Which first-party service will protect your application from DDoS?

   A. Security and Command Center.

   B. Cloudflare.

   C. Cloud Sentinel.

   D. Cloud Armor.

10. You have a multi-terabyte dataset you want to migrate to Google Cloud and would prefer to do it via hardware. What is your best option?

   A. Transfer Appliance.

   B. Online transfer.

   C. Work with a partner.

   D. None of the above.

Key

Part 1

1. A. A way to virtually host servers and applications.

2. C. Control.

3. A. Shared responsibility model.

4. C. Offload security responsibilities to a third party.

5. D. Infrastructure as a Service.

6. A. When an application is delivered directly to end users over the internet.

7. B. A private cloud is dedicated to one organization while a public cloud is shared between multiple organizations.

8. C. When an organization has both on-premises and cloud infrastructure.

9. D. None of the above.

10. D. All of the above.

11. B. Hybrid.

12. B. Cloud, cloud-native.

13. D. All of the above.

14. A. Total cost of ownership.

15. A. Regions and zones, with each region having multiple zones.

16. C. To translate websites into IP addresses and route the traffic accordingly.

17. A. True.

18. A. The customer.

19. B. The PaaS provider.

20. A. The customer.

Part 2

1. B. Pub/Sub.

2. A. Cloud Storage.

3. D. Data Catalog.

4. D. Looker.

5. D. A data transformation tool based on Apache Beam.

6. C. BigQuery.

7. A. Vertex AI Platform.

8. D. All of the above.

9. D. All of the above.

10. B. Apache Spark.

11. D. All of the above.

12. C. Snowflake.

13. D. A and B.

14. A. Spanner.

15. D. All of the above.

16. B. Vertex AI Notebooks.

17. D. CloudSQL.

18. B. Leverage BigQuery's native ML capability – BQML.

19. A. **Natural Language Processing (NLP)**.

20. C. Vertex Search and Conversation.

21. D. Google Cloud Compute Engine.

22. B. A service that allows for the number of VMs to scale up and down based on load.

23. C. Apigee.

24. D. Google Cloud delivering managed Kubernetes as a service to customers.

25. C. A and B.

26. D. All of the above.

27. D. A and C.

28. D. All of the above.

29. A. App Engine.

30. D. Cloud Run.

31. A. An enterprise-grade way for managing permissions and access to data.

32. C. Kubernetes Engine.

33. B. Compute Engine.

34. A. App Engine.

35. D. Cloud Run.

36. A. Cloud Functions.

37. B. CloudSQL.

38. A. Lift and shift.

39. B. Transform then shift.

40. A. A way to define who is responsible for what part of the technology stack when leveraging cloud providers.

41. D. A measure of how often a system is up and running.

42. B. A measure of how often a system is reachable and usable.

43. C. 99.999%.

44. B. Five minutes.

45. C. 50 minutes.

46. A. When an attacker copies legitimate artifacts to try and trick someone into divulging secrets via the web or email.

47. A. Nation-state attackers.

48. A. A Contractual obligation designating a level of uptime and reliability to customers.

49. C. An internal metric used to measure progress toward a designated uptime goal.

50. B. An internal goal for designating a target level of uptime and reliability.

51. D. It defines a set of practices for maximizing developer productivity.

52. A. It defines a set of practices for maximizing service reliability.

53. C. It provides data and metrics for measuring system health and performance.

54. D. Cloud Monitoring.

55. B. Service account.

56. C. Org > Folder > Project > Resource.

57. D. Security and Command Center.

58. B. A way for Google to do MFA on server-side infrastructure.

59. C. Something you ask.

60. D. All of the above.

Part 3

Scenario 1 – E-Commerce

1. D. All of the above.

2. D. Cloud Run.

3. B. Reallocate resources.

4. C. CloudSQL.

5. B. Cloud Storage as a data lake.

6.   A. Dataproc.

7.   D. BigQuery.

8.   C. A and B.

9.   B. Vision/Video.

10. A. Natural Language.

Scenario 2 – Healthcare

1.   D. HIPAA.

2.   B. Apigee.

3.   B. Bigtable.

4.   C. Google Cloud offers indemnification for those using their first-party models.

5.   A. Google Cloud does not review nor retain customer prompts and responses.

6.   A. Vertex AI platform.

7.   D. Speech to Text.

8.   C. Claude.

9.   D. Cloud Armor.

10. A. Transfer Appliance.

Index

U

V

W

packtpub.com

Subscribe to our online digital library for full access to over 7,000 books and videos, as well as industry leading tools to help you plan your personal development and advance your career. For more information, please visit our website.

Why subscribe?

- Spend less time learning and more time coding with practical eBooks and Videos from over 4,000 industry professionals

- Improve your learning with Skill Plans built especially for you

- Get a free eBook or video every month

- Fully searchable for easy access to vital information

- Copy and paste, print, and bookmark content

Did you know that Packt offers eBook versions of every book published, with PDF and ePub files available? You can upgrade to the eBook version at packtpub.com and as a print book customer, you are entitled to a discount on the eBook copy. Get in touch with us at customercare@packtpub.com for more details.

At www.packtpub.com, you can also read a collection of free technical articles, sign up for a range of free newsletters, and receive exclusive discounts and offers on Packt books and eBooks.

Other Books You May Enjoy

If you enjoyed this book, you may be interested in these other books by Packt:

Google Cloud for Developers

Hector Parra Martinez

ISBN: 978-1-83763-074-5

- Understand how to write, run, and troubleshoot code on Google Cloud
- Choose between serverless or GKE containers for running your code
- Connect your code to Google Cloud services using public APIs
- Migrate your code to Google Cloud flawlessly
- Build hybrid cloud solutions that can run virtually anywhere
- Get to grips with Cloud Functions, App Engine, GKE, and Anthos

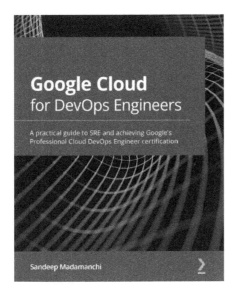

Google Cloud for DevOps Engineers

Sandeep Madamanchi

ISBN: 978-1-83921-801-9

- Categorize user journeys and explore different ways to measure SLIs
- Explore the four golden signals for monitoring a user-facing system
- Understand psychological safety along with other SRE cultural practices
- Create containers with build triggers and manual invocations
- Delve into Kubernetes workloads and potential deployment strategies
- Secure GKE clusters via private clusters, Binary Authorization, and shielded GKE nodes
- Get to grips with monitoring, Metrics Explorer, uptime checks, and alerting
- Discover how logs are ingested via the Cloud Logging API

Packt is searching for authors like you

If you're interested in becoming an author for Packt, please visit `authors.packtpub.com` and apply today. We have worked with thousands of developers and tech professionals, just like you, to help them share their insight with the global tech community. You can make a general application, apply for a specific hot topic that we are recruiting an author for, or submit your own idea.

Share Your Thoughts

Now you've finished *Google Cloud Digital Leader Certification Guide*, we'd love to hear your thoughts! Scan the QR code below to go straight to the Amazon review page for this book and share your feedback or leave a review on the site that you purchased it from.

`https://packt.link/r/1805129619`

Your review is important to us and the tech community and will help us make sure we're delivering excellent quality content.

Download a free PDF copy of this book

Thanks for purchasing this book!

Do you like to read on the go but are unable to carry your print books everywhere?

Is your eBook purchase not compatible with the device of your choice?

Don't worry, now with every Packt book you get a DRM-free PDF version of that book at no cost.

Read anywhere, any place, on any device. Search, copy, and paste code from your favorite technical books directly into your application.

The perks don't stop there, you can get exclusive access to discounts, newsletters, and great free content in your inbox daily

Follow these simple steps to get the benefits:

1. Scan the QR code or visit the link below

https://packt.link/free-ebook/978-1-80512-961-5

2. Submit your proof of purchase
3. That's it! We'll send your free PDF and other benefits to your email directly

www.ingramcontent.com/pod-product-compliance
Lightning Source LLC
Chambersburg PA
CBHW080526060326
40690CB00022B/5044